D0244699

Blinded by the Sun

A play

Stephen Poliakoff

Samuel French — London
New York - Toronto - Hollywood

© 1996 BY STEPHEN POLIAKOFF

Rights of Performance by Amateurs are controlled by Samuel French Ltd, 52 Fitzroy Street, London W1T 5JR, and they, or their authorized agents, issue licences to amateurs on payment of a fee. **It is an infringement of the Copyright to give any performance or public reading of the play before the fee has been paid and the licence issued.**

The Royalty Fee indicated below is subject to contract and subject to variation at the sole discretion of Samuel French Ltd.

Basic fee for each and every
performance by amateurs Code M
in the British Isles

The Professional Rights in this play are controlled by Judy Daish Associates Ltd, 2 St Charles Place. London, W10 6EG

The publication of this play does not imply that it is necessarily available for performance by amateurs or professionals, either in the British Isles or Overseas. Amateurs and professionals considering a production are strongly advised in their own interests to apply to the appropriate agents for written consent before starting rehearsals or booking a theatre or hall.

ISBN 0 573 01929 0

Please see page iv for further copyright information

BLINDED BY THE SUN

First performed in the Cottesloe auditorium of the Royal
National Theatre, London, on 28th August 1996, with the
following cast:

Al	Douglas Hodge
Elinor	Frances de la Tour
Christopher	Duncan Bell
Joanna	Indra Ové
Professor	Graham Crowden
Ghislane	Orla Brady
Barbara	Hermione Norris
Charlie	Walter Sparrow

Directed by **Ron Daniels**
Designed by **Tom Piper**
Lighting by **Rich Fisher**
Sound by **Simon Baker**

Other plays by Stephen Poliakoff published by
Samuel French Ltd

Breaking the Silence
City Sugar
Hitting Town

ACT I

SCENE 1

The stage is framed by pale green walls. The paint has faded. There is a crumbling emblem on the back wall, dedicating the building to the Sciences, dating back to Edwardian times. The effect is of a once splendid, rather confident space, now decaying very slightly. Bench seats run along one side of the stage, on one is a cup of tea and a tin of ginger biscuits. On the wall above the bench is an old tannoy. A row of full-length old wooden lockers is on the other side. An old-fashioned soft drinks machine, dating from the mid-Sixties, sits in the corner, brash and incongruous

Al is facing out. He is forty years old, with a beady, humorous manner

Al The first thing I ought to say is—I will try to tell this fairly. Although, clearly, I will always have the last word. (*He moves*) Luckily. (*He smiles*) But I will try—quite hard—not to paint too sympathetic a portrait of myself. (*He moves casually round the stage*) This is pretty much, I think, how it happened. (*He opens one of the lockers. It is full of transparent plastic bags, like scene-of-the-crime plastic bags*) And to help me remember, there are these. (*He surveys the bags*) Maybe a slightly creepy way of keeping a diary, but surprisingly effective in bottling the past. They look a little disgusting, I know, all bunched up, but individually they're fine, (*He smiles*) And not nearly as odd as they seem. (*He takes one out and stares at it for a second*) Inside, some of the objects that seemed important *at the time*, to help remember that particular day. Some very obvious ... like this bag from around the middle of what happened—in it a faded colour supplement. (*He smiles*) We made the cover! (*He holds the unopened bag up to the light*) I'll open it when we get to it—but if I remember right, "A science detective story, a tale of greed, deception, jealousy, and a touch of hate, in the unlikely setting of the chemistry department of a northern university". A little sensational of course. (*He throws it back into the locker, then turns*) Actually, it's even better than that! (*He opens the first locker and takes out another bag and a jacket that is hanging there. He changes jackets*) So the first one I'm going to use is from the day I knew there was a good chance I was going to be terminated. (*He rips open the bag*) A cinema ticket. I have no idea why that is here—sometimes one

Christopher exits

Elinor Goodness, I've got to get on too. (*She gets up*) Just offer to tidy up
his office, Albie, if all else fails. It'll be *fine*. (*She peers into the biscuit tin*)
I think I'll take another one of these. Super.

Elinor exits

Joanna (*imitating Elinor*) "Super".
Al (*watching Elinor go*) No—you should try to get some time with her. She's
a very distinguished lady.
Joanna Is she?
Al Oh, yes, she was closely involved in the discovery of the structure of
vitamins, when she was very young. (*He smiles*) She taught me. She's
marvellous.
Joanna What were all those knowing looks for?
Al (*innocently*) Which looks? Oh—I'm about to be summoned into an
important interview.
Joanna Your friend seemed very sure you had a lot more time to spare than
him.
Al It's the truth. I do. (*Genuinely*) Christopher's very good, he's published
a lot.
Joanna And you?
Al We'll come to me later!

Pause

(*Smiling*) Actually, there's a very strong chance I'm about to be sacked.
Joanna (*very startled*) What? Now?
Al Yes. Any moment. (*He watches her*) And *you*—it's very unusual to see
a history student here. So what is your thesis on, Joanna?

Silence

Joanna The impact of the invention of detergent on public health.

Slight pause

Al That's a good idea!
Joanna You're kidding? Most people are usually speechless when I tell
them.
Al No, no, it's good. History of how washing has changed—quite a sexy
subject. Sanitation ... poverty ... whether people live or die. (*He smiles*)
What's more, there's very little competition.

Joanna That's why I chose it.
Al Precisely.

Pause

Joanna (*looking straight at him*) Why did they think you'd automatically have time for me?

Al hesitates

You usually have time for young female graduates, is that it?

Slight pause

Al Always. Absolutely. (*He smiles*) Is it that obvious?
Professor (*off*) Albert!
Al Here we go.
Joanna (*moving to exit*) It's OK, go on. The History of Detergent can wait…

Joanna exits

Al is alone on stage for a second

A large desk comes on, papers leaking out of its drawers

The Professor enters and stands with his back to Al. The Professor is a tall crisp man in his seventies

Silence

Professor So what are we going to do with you, Albert?
Al (*quietly*) Oh, shit.
Professor What did you say?
Al I said quite—that's a very reasonable question.
Professor Certain atmosphere of decay, wouldn't you agree, around this place? Even the buildings look disgusting, shabby. And this is a great department, with a distinguished history. (*He turns*) I don't suppose you think of death very often, Albert?
Al I … I try to keep it to a sensible minimum.
Professor Did I tell you I was giving up this job?
Al (*watchfully*) No.
Professor But it's not a surprise?
Al Not … in so many words.

Professor Don't be so mealy-mouthed, Albert, this is not the time. I'm seventy-two and feel older. I'm becoming Inactive Emeritus Professor. Wonderful title, isn't it? Inactive! Thank God. This will be in a few weeks.

Al As soon as that?

Professor Yes. Who do you think should succeed me?

Al That's not an easy question.

Professor (*sharply*) Isn't it?

Al (*exasperated*) Well, maybe for you it is.

Professor Now—and I want to feel you're being honest, Albert, how about Christopher?

Al Christopher, certainly—that makes a lot of sense. (*After a very slight pause*) An obvious choice.

Professor Yes, *but*? (*Impatiently, very formidably*) Come on, Albert, tell me! (*He stares straight at him*)

Al (*tentatively*) Well, the only question is, will he be off soon? He is working in a high profile area, at some stage he'll be tremendously in demand. Is this too small a pond for him?

Professor Yes. And now—Elinor?

Al Of course, Elinor should get it—if she wants it. Her record is unchallengeable clearly, her great reputation.

Professor But? (*Sharply*) Come on, but?

Al She's deep in her work, of course. The only question is—would she really like it? But if she——

Professor I know all about Elinor, we go back a long time.

Al Then there's Hayward, of course, Bogle, and Beattie ... even Warhurst. And we should advertise, we could go outside...

Professor Take too long. The situation is too urgent. (*He moves*) All the rest of the department are third raters. Dead meat. (*He turns. After a pause*) I want you to do it, Albert.

Silence

Al What? (*Stunned*) I don't think you can mean it.

Professor (*coldly*) What did I say?

Al I thought you said I should do it.

Professor And why are you so surprised by that?

Al Naturally, I'm a little stunned. I'm not sure it's being realistic.

Professor Why?

Al Because ... because my reputation compared to the others, my track record, is a little thin.

Professor Certainly there's no distinction there, a modest record. In fact, sometimes I seriously doubt you're a true scientist at all.

Al That's what I'm trying to say.

Professor No, you're something much more valuable, and much rarer—a born administrator.

Al (*startled*) I've been doing a little admin for you, but...

Professor It comes effortlessly to you. We've had buckets full of distinction with me being here, and *look where it has got us*! The department is profoundly unfashionable. It will always exist, of course, because of its history. But it needs somebody who can re-invent it.

Al (*mumbling*) Don't do this ... don't do it.

Professor What are you mumbling?

Al Maybe Elinor's expecting it. She should be offered first——

Professor (*cutting him off*) Elinor must be left alone to complete her latest research. And Christopher too. You yourself gave reasons why they shouldn't do it.

Al I didn't! I didn't mean I should get it instead!

Professor (*staring at Al*) The Vice-Chancellor agrees with me. And the Appointments Committee is also happy. I hope you're not going to refuse, Albert.... I don't think that would be particularly wise.

Pause

Al No, I'm not refusing.

Professor I told you, it wasn't a difficult question.

Al (*very quietly*) It's an honour. Thank you.

Professor Honour has nothing to do with it. The official announcement will be made tomorrow. That will be all, Albert.

Al Are you going to tell them? Elinor and Christopher. Explain it to them.

Professor (*surprised*) Me? Certainly not! *You* start doing everything, as from now.

Professor exits

Al is alone. He steps away from the desk

Al Oh Jesus! (*His head goes back, handkerchief up to his nose*)

Joanna enters, slowly, eating chocolate

Al sees her after a second, out of the corner of his eye

You're still here!

Joanna So it appears.

Al (*smiling*) I didn't expect that.

Joanna I just had to know what happened. Are *you* still here?

Al It's not that simple. I can't tell you yet. (*His head goes back*) Sometimes when things get complicated I get a nosebleed ... it's just a few specks really.

Elinor and Christopher enter

Christopher You see, he's out already. I told you it wouldn't be long.
Al (*half turning*) It didn't take long, no.
Elinor (*seeing the handkerchief as she gets closer*) Blood! Oh, Albert—it's not that bad, is it?
Al No, I'm OK. (*He faces Elinor and Christopher*) At least for the moment.
Christopher So what happened?
Al Brownhill is leaving.
Christopher At last! (*Buzzing with the news*) I don't believe it!
Elinor Good. That's good. We've been waiting for that.
Christopher And he told Al first! When is he going?
Al Almost immediately. (*He moves*) Now, nobody say this is a joke—*don't* say "you're joking, of course". OK? (*He stops and pauses*) But he's recommending ... for some reason ... God knows why, but ... he's arranged to give his job—to *me*.

Silence

Elinor Albie—he didn't!
Christopher Jesus. No.
Al Yes! (*With a self-mocking smile*) Amazing, isn't it?
Christopher (*grinning*) For once you've really surprised me.
Al *You're* surprised! I want to say right from the start, it's purely for administrative reasons. They want the true creative minds to be free, unencumbered, for their research.

Pause

Say something.

Pause

At least it's the devil you know.

Silence

Elinor (*crisply*) I think it's possibly a very sensible move. Good.
Christopher (*with a charming smile*) We'll have to make appointments to see Al. Form a queue, outside his door.

Al No, no, *no*. It won't be like that. Quite the reverse. We'll all plan together.
Elinor (*lightly*) Albie! Head of the Department! (*She pauses*) Don't worry,
we understand. (*She moves up to him*) There is no problem. (*She gives him
a little kiss*) You'll make a very satisfactory professor, I'm sure.

Elinor exits

Christopher and Al look at each other

Christopher Now the shock's worn off. Yes—Elinor's right. It could be
very useful. (*He smiles*) And it'll certainly be interesting. (*Pleasantly*)
You're much better suited to all that admin than I am. (*He moves*) You see,
you were wrong about Wednesdays.
Al I'm not so sure!
Christopher (*making to leave, indicating Joanna, in a low voice*) That was
quick work, even by your standards, Al.

Christopher leaves

Al is alone on stage with Joanna

Joanna Wow!
Al Wow, yes.
Joanna It's great, isn't it?
Al You don't understand. (*He pauses for a moment*) I say this as a scientist,
a realist, not out of false modesty I assure you, but because of the *facts*. (*He
turns*) Christopher is really good, a star, and Elinor, of course, is Elinor.
And I'm…
Joanna And you?
Al And I'm pint-sized. A true hack.
Joanna Are you? It's still fantastic. (*She laughs*) Strange and fantastic.
Al (*smiling*) It's a bloody nightmare.

Black-out

SCENE 2

*Al is alone on stage. He takes his jacket off and drapes it on a chair. He closes
the drawers of the desk. He peers at the bag he has selected—then rips it open.
Inside are some coloured paper strips*

Al And so now we come to these. They look quite innocent—like paper
chains … but they were a considerable mistake.

Al exits with the bag

Joanna enters, carrying her sneakers and her shoulder bag, and sits on the edge of the desk. She is barefoot, her clothes slightly askew. She is buttoning her blouse up, the last few buttons

Barbara enters. She is in her early twenties, with an abrasive manner, and a Lancashire accent. She stops, very surprised to see Joanna sitting on the desk

Barbara Oh! I thought there was about to be a meeting. I must have made a mistake.

Joanna (*not completely concealing what she's been doing*) No. There *is* a meeting. I was just leaving. (*Unabashed*) Mr Golfar has been kind enough … to glance at some of my work. (*With a slight smile*) My research.

Barbara *Professor* Golfar.

Joanna Yes, of course, Professor Golfar.

Barbara Easy mistake to make. (*She stares at Joanna*) I'm sorry. I thought seeing somebody like you here, there *couldn't* be a meeting.

Joanna (*amused*) Somebody like me.

Barbara A visitor—from outside the department. (*She moves*) I work with Dr Lathwell, and we've been asked to attend a meeting at precisely two o'clock. It is now two-oh-two. Elinor, Dr Brickman, has also been asked. They are both very busy people.

Joanna Of course. (*She puts on her sneakers*) I'll be as quick as I can, I promise.

Pause. Barbara watches her

Barbara Amazing to think that in this room one of the first conversations about the creation of radar happened. (*She touches the desk*) *Right* here. And now…

Joanna And now you've come right down in the world—you're stuck with Professor Golfar.

Barbara Did I say that? (*Very sharply*) I certainly didn't hear myself say that.

Joanna (*surprised by Barbara's self-possession*) No. You didn't.

Elinor enters

Elinor Oh, I thought there was a meeting.

Joanna (*putting on the other shoe hurriedly*) I was just explaining, I'm not here, I'm *really* not here.

Christopher enters and sees Joanna

Christopher (*breezily*) That's a delightful surprise. There is no meeting—
the meeting's been cancelled! I can get back.

Al enters, holding cardboard charts under his arm

Al No, no, no. There *is* a meeting. Joanna was just on the point of leaving.
Joanna (*laughing*) Don't worry—I'm out of here! (*She stops by the exit*)
Thank you for your time, Professor Golfar. It's been very useful.
Al Absolutely. I'll await the next instalment with interest.

Joanna exits. She has left her shoulder bag

Joanna! (*He turns*) I'll deal with that later.

Christopher laughs at this. Al looks at him unabashed

Her work's good.
Christopher (*amused*) Of course, Al. It's great that you can find the time.
Al (*smiling broadly*) Yes, I know, isn't it! (*He looks across the room at them*)

*The atmosphere is suddenly more formal, as Elinor, Christopher and
Barbara wait for him to speak*

Please sit. Come on, everyone!
Elinor We'll stand, I think. This won't take long, will it?
Al No, no, of course not. (*He nervously shuffles papers for a moment, not
facing them directly*) You should see some of the things I've found in his
desk!
Elinor So why have you summoned us all here, Albie?
Al (*laughing*) I haven't summoned you, for Chrissake! This is an informal
gathering.
Christopher Why did you need to see us, Al?
Al OK, OK, I would prefer this to be more relaxed, but still… (*He looks
across at them*) Jesus! This is not exactly easy for me. To address you…
(*He pauses*) OK—I'm diving in *now*. You see these strips… (*He lays out
coloured strips along the desk*)
Elinor Strips!
Al If you're red, Elinor, and Christopher's green…
Elinor I'm a red paper strip?
Al Yes, yes, just for today. And then we look here… (*He indicates the chart*)
Over the last two years at the amount of *teaching* the red and green strips
have done. (*He holds up the big chart*)

There is very little sign of any red or green

Elinor I don't need to look at any chart to know that, Albie.
Al No. It's just with all due respect to Bogle, Beattie and Warhurst, we have a priceless asset in the two of you, Christopher, (*to Elinor*) and you ... you're star status, your great reputation, Elinor. (*He swallows deeply*) So, in order to attract more students in the future, which we must do, I want— I would very much like—you to teach more, to do more bread-and-butter lectures. (*With the chart*) To have a little more red here ... and green there.

Silence

Elinor The answer is no, Albie.
Al (*with the display*) I just want to show——
Elinor (*calmly*) The answer is no. I have always taught once a week, for the last twenty-five years.
Christopher (*effortlessly*) There are other priorities, Al—the answer has to be *no*. (*Crisply*) Is that it?

Silence

Barbara Can we go?
Al (*with another deep breath*) I was also considering—see what you think of this—to help us with sponsorship from industry ... when we want to target a little of our research ... renaming the department, "Energy Studies". (*His voice tails away*) As has happened elsewhere.

Silence

Elinor I don't like that very much, Albie, I have to confess.
Al No? (*He looks across at them*) I'll keep thinking.

They begin to move. Al coughs

And there's the room.
Elinor (*sharply*) The room?
Al I was just wondering, Elinor, if there was any chance, because we need to enlarge the computer room, of having a corner ... a fragment of the space you occupy.

Silence

Elinor From my lab? No, Albie, that is not open to negotiation.
Al Not open! (*He smiles nervously*) It was worth a try, wasn't it?
Elinor I'm not sure it was, no.

Pause. Al mock-strangles himself with the paper strips

Al OK, I get the idea!
Christopher (*easily, making for the exit*) Al, I'm drawing up a list of other
things I think you can help us with, OK? I'm sure you'll agree to them.
Come on, Barbara. (*Pleasantly*) No more Energy Studies please.

Christopher exits with Barbara

Barbara No!
Al (*to Elinor*) Do you have to go?

Elinor stops

I made a mess of it, didn't I? (*He laughs*) Don't know what possessed me
to do a visual presentation—to you!
Elinor There is no need to try so hard, Albie, there's not such a hurry.
Al (*very respectfully*) No. You're right, Elinor.
Elinor (*smiling*) Of course I am. (*She indicates Joanna's bag*) You're still
finding opportunity to enjoy yourself I see.
Al For the moment, yes.
Elinor Does she know you're married?
Al (*amused*) Elinor! I'm *not* married. Kathy and I—we're estranged.
Elinor I thought you said you were working very hard on getting together
again.
Al Yes, we are. (*With Joanna's bag, poking around noisily*) Just occasionally
that gets interrupted.
Elinor (*laughing*) I see. Don't you dare go through her things, Albie, really!
Stop it!
Al (*reluctantly putting the bag down*) I can't be like Christopher, beautiful
lawyer wife ... golden romantic couple ... faithful. (*He indicates Joanna's
belongings*) This is what I'm like.
Elinor Yes. (*Lightly*) And not forgetting those odd plastic bags you keep
things in. Time to give those up too, isn't it?
Al No, no, I can't!
Elinor (*lightly*) You'll grow up sooner or later.
Al Don't bank on it!

Pause. Elinor moves

Elinor There we are, then. Super. (*She turns*) I ought to tell you, my work's
reaching a *very* important stage.
Al (*very respectfully*) Of course, Elinor. (*Then casually*) Is this the work on

mutant haemoglobin or is there something else, entirely new, you are working on as well?

Elinor That was a good try. When I'm ready, Albie.

Al (*smiling*) You know going through the records I was amazed to see how many invitations you get from all over the world.

Elinor You mean still.

Al I didn't mean still! Would I ever say that? No! (*Impressed*) And you don't accept any of them.

Elinor Well, they're easy to refuse—I find I don't like flying any more.

Al Really?

Elinor Which is funny, because when I was young, I always seemed to be flying places, often in rickety planes, turning somersaults in thunderstorms. (*She looks across at him*) So, Albie, you understand the situation—there must be no mention again, about changing my arrangements. At all.

Al I promise, Elinor. An absolute promise. (*He smiles suddenly*) There's one condition.

Elinor (*very formidably*) Which is?

Al (*warmly*) You let me get you out of your lab for one evening.

Elinor (*with a startled laugh*) No, no, I don't think so!

Al (*coaxingly*) Oh yes, just for once. Here you are, tucked away, living on the campus, shutting out all trivial distractions—when did you last even go into town?

Elinor (*joking*) Quite recently! Sometime in the last five years I'm sure.

Al We'll go with Christopher. All talk about work will be strictly forbidden.

Elinor That sounds promising.

Al We could celebrate your birthday.

Elinor (*lightly*) I'm not sure I want to be reminded of my birthday. (*She moves*) Well, if you can find something surprising, Albie...

Al Surprising? (*With a teasing smile*) You mean, something crude and low down?

Elinor I'm not sure about that! (*She moves, then turns. Breezily*) And if I do come, I'm free of your interference for ever?

Al Yes.

Elinor (*lightly, moving to exit*) You might just have a deal, Albie!

Elinor exits, leaving Al alone on stage

The Lights change. Shopping-mall muzak comes up in the background. Neon light springs to life along the back wall. Al is holding a third plastic bag— he opens it. He takes out a glass

Al One milkshake ... the glass still stained with apricot flavour ... a trifle caramelized now ... a little lipstick visible on the straw. (*He smiles*) This

is our trip down town. (*He moves, then turns*) An equation—possibly—
begins to form.

Black-out

SCENE 3

The neon light. Muzak

*Al is standing with a Virtual Reality headset on. He is next to the black metal
VR car with its joystick, but he is standing rather than sitting in it*

*Christopher, Joanna and Elinor are sitting on shopping-mall chairs.
Christopher and Joanna both have milkshakes. Elinor is rolling a thin
cigarette*

*Behind them can be heard the intermittent sound of jackpots being paid out
and the sound of the games in the amusement arcade. The sudden, heavy,
pulsating noise of money pouring out. Al's head flicks as he experiences the
VR images, the others watching him, calling out to him*

Al Yes, yes ... it's getting a little faster! (*He gropes sideways for the joystick*)
Low, really *low*.
Christopher So what is it?
Joanna What are you seeing, Al?
Elinor (*calmly rolling a cigarette*) Maybe we shouldn't ask.
Christopher (*grinning*) Getting to the more explicit parts now, are we?
Al No! No, hardly. (*His head is moving*)
Joanna This is a family shopping mall, after all!
Elinor (*smoking*) I hate the word "mall".
Al No, no, I'm moving across a sort of idyllic landscape. Just brushing the
top of an English water meadow.
Christopher (*disbelieving*) Oh yeah?
Al Now I'm skimming along a river ... big fish, teeth coming at me ... girls
sunbathing on the bank, dreamily sucking a piece of grass, as I go by.
Christopher (*patronising, but affectionate*) There we are, we knew it.
Elinor He's probably seeing something totally different!
Al (*taking the headset off*) Come here, Elinor, you must have a turn, while
it's still running.
Elinor No, I can imagine it, Albie.
Al (*tempting, coaxing her*) Come on, just for information.
Elinor (*getting up*) OK, for you ... just a peep.

Al takes the headset, places it gently over Elinor's eyes

Christopher Trust a group of scientists to be the *last* people to try out Virtual
   Reality.
Al (*as he slips the headset on*) And you have to give it at least thirty seconds,
   OK?

*Elinor holds her head erect, headset on, not sitting in the vehicle, standing
a little apart from it, the cable snaking behind her*

Elinor Oh my God, no, Albie! Really! You liar! You cheat!
Christopher (*smiling*) What is it? What have you done, Al?
Joanna What have you made her look at?

Elinor is alone, c

Elinor Jeepers creepers! It's flying, high speed flying. I seem to be in the
   cockpit of something doing several thousand miles an hour.
Al (*beaming*) It's called Flight Deck 2010.
Elinor (*moving with the headset, groping for controls*) At this precise
   moment … we seem to be heading straight for the side of a rather large
   mountain. (*She yanks the stick*) It's going to be close. Just pulled up in time!
   (*She laughs*) This isn't very subtle, Albie! (*She moves to lift the headset off*)
   Shock therapy, for my fear of flying?
Al No, no, wait! Don't take it off yet. Please—see where it takes you next!

Elinor keeps it on, her head going back. Her figure tilts forward a little

Elinor We're diving—Geronimo! Hurtling … right into the middle of a very
   tall building. Going to hit the glass——
Al (*laughing*) It shatters!
Elinor *Now*! Hold on everyone—we're roaring over the office furniture.
Al (*to Christopher*) You should have a go.
Christopher (*with a charming smile*) Don't need to. I've worn those before.
   I think it's strange how *crude* computer graphics still are, not remotely
   virtually real.
Al (*grinning*) It's not good enough for you. Of course! (*He turns*)

Elinor is standing, her headset at an odd angle, her body slowly descending

   Elinor, what's happening?

No answer

Christopher Elinor, are you all right?

Elinor What? (*She lifts the headset off*) We were just going down a drain in the middle of the road in New York. (*She smiles, leaving the headset lying on stage*)

The sound of money pouring out of arcade machines

Thank you, Albie.

Joanna (*putting the headset on*) Is it still running?

Al You wanted a surprise. It needed to be something you'd never normally do.

Sirens sound in the distance, mingling with the muzak

(*Taking the headset*) What would you like to see if this machine could show you anything?

Elinor *Anything?*

Al Yes, you know ... like, like ... playing back your first sexual experience.

Elinor Oh, I see! (*Immediately*) I think that's quite an easy choice; it'd be wonderful to go into one's childhood and see exact reproductions of the landscapes and people one remembers, but do *different* things there, be good at everything one was bad at, have a Virtually Real *alternative* childhood.

Al Yes, yes, that's a better idea!

Christopher takes the headset calmly

Christopher Or an even better idea——

Al (*quietly*) Even better?

Christopher (*effortlessly*) Yes. *Enter other people's past.* And be able to move around there without being spotted, seeing all the things they haven't been telling you, whom they really slept with, and when. How they *actually* behaved.

Elinor (*smiling to herself*) That's nice, yes.

Al tries to keep up with them, with their ideas

Al Yes, it'd be tremendous to go into your past, Elinor, be there as a witness!

Elinor (*surprised*) Really? I don't think so.

Al Oh yes, definitely. Seeing you when you were starting out, a young woman.

Elinor (*laughing*) He's doing it again! I don't believe it. Reminding me of my age!

The sound of arcade machines, money pouring out

Al No, no, *no*. When you were working with the old monsters, doing your great work with Barker-Wyatt.

Christopher Yes, *I* wouldn't mind being able to go back and watch you bossing them all around.

Al This young girl (*he smiles at Elinor*) burning with conviction, with almost religious fervour, setting these older men such high standards!

Elinor They always called me the "female prodigy", like something out of Dickens! I can still feel their fat hands when I think about them—they used to give me these little taps on the shoulder——

Joanna Did you go on picnics?

They look up. They've forgotten about her

Elinor (*surprised*) Picnics?

Joanna Yes. (*With a slight laugh*) You know I always imagine boffins on picnics with their bicycles lying around in heaps, and you all playing cricket with hard-boiled eggs.

They look at each other

As you talk brilliant science.

Al indicates the clamour of burglar alarms in the distance

Al This is our version tonight. An urban picnic!

Elinor Yes, you're right. We *did* have our picnics. They talked, and I sunbathed a few yards away.

Al (*suddenly loud*) Oh, I'd love to have seen that. You on the grass, long hair stretched out, driving them mad!

Elinor (*lightly, smoking*) I wasn't particularly successful at doing that, I promise you.

Al (*loudly, intensely*) I really do wish I'd been there!

Pause. They look at him in surprise. The urban night sounds are all around

So... (*He moves, picking up the headset*) Let's have another programme to see us on our way. (*He grins*) How about, swimming with dolphins?

Christopher (*calmly*) No, Al. I don't think I can stay here any longer. Burglar alarms! Amusement arcades! It's too depressing.

Al (*grinning*) I quite like it.

Christopher Oh, come on, it's truly pathetic. Trying to imitate a corner of

Piccadilly Circus—as if the original wasn't tacky enough. This town is
never going to recover, it's like the university...
Al I'm not *that* pessimistic.
Christopher (*smiling*) Well, you're running the department, Al, you have
to be a little more optimistic, and that's good.
Al (*grinning*) Much prefer to be in America, would you?

During the following, Joanna picks up the VR headset

Christopher (*lightly*) I'm not sure... I certainly don't spend my time lusting
after a lucrative position in the States——
Joanna (*suddenly*) What if this could show you the future?

They look at her

If you could put a coin in and it'd show you yourself in a few years' time,
for five minutes ... what would you see?
Christopher Oh, that old chestnut...
Al Yes, what will happen to us three?
Joanna Oh, thanks!
Al Four, of course. (*He grins*) I said four.
Joanna Like hell you did!

Pause. The sound of the amusement arcade and burglar alarms

Elinor I'll be in exactly the same place, no doubt, wearing the same clothes.
Al That sounds right. I'll be bustling round the department, still trying to get
its name changed.
Joanna (*laughing*) I'll hope I'll be doing something original and provocative.
And earning money! (*She turns*) Christopher?

They look at him. Pause

Christopher (*smiling, calmly*) I'm not telling.
Al ⎱ (*together*) Come on! Cheat!
Joanna ⎰
Elinor You mean you know! If you're not *telling*, you must know.

Slight pause

Christopher (*calmly*) I'd like not to be here. (*He smiles*) But I probably will
be.
Al (*grinning*) Aha. Something's brewing! (*He lifts the headset, covers his*

eyes for a moment) No. Nothing's visible ... the future cannot be glimpsed tonight. (*Amiably, as he resets the headset in the VR car, to Elinor*) You know if you gave me the cupboard room, that little bit of your lab I need for the extension, we'd probably have room for one of these at work. Could nip in for a quick fix at tea time!

Silence

Elinor (*very steely, angrily*) I wish you hadn't said that, Albie. Don't start talking about that now—*understand*?
Al It was a joke, I...
Elinor No, it wasn't. (*She suddenly looks straight at him*) So that's the point of this evening, is it?
Al What you mean, the point?
Elinor The *point*, Albie. To get me relaxed, soften me up—isn't that the current expression, so you can start persuading me to give up some of my lab space. That's the true agenda of the evening.
Al Of course it's not.
Elinor I would take a very dim view indeed if that's what you were up to.
Christopher I thought all those plans were dead, Al.
Al Yes it was just a stupid remark, a bad joke.
Elinor Yes, it was. I will *not* have you interfering.
Al (*very flustered*) I promised you, I wouldn't. OK. You've got to believe me. (*He moves*) Shit! This is getting messy. One of those moments you want the ground to swallow you up. I don't want your birthday spoilt!
Elinor Well, if you've forgotten your plans, I've forgotten what just happened. (*Icily*) But that better be the case.
Al Yes, of course. Come on, Joanna, we'll bring the car round. Give a moment for things to cool. (*He makes to leave*) Fuck! I want this to be such a good evening. Erase the last few minutes, *please*, they never happened.

Al exits with Joanna

Pause

Elinor Dear Albie, he still needs house training.
Christopher He means well. He's just rather clumsy about it.
Elinor I certainly hope he means well.
Christopher Of course. This is *Al*, for Chrissake. What can he do to us? He worships you, you know.
Elinor (*startled*) Worships...? No.
Christopher Oh, yes. He's in awe of you, Elinor. Of *course*. Always has been. He'll never cause us any problems. (*He smiles*) What's more, it may cease to matter.

Elinor Oh, yes? (*She looks at him*) That sounds nice and mysterious.
Christopher Something I've been working on for quite a while… I'm not
saying any more now. (*With a charming smile*) But just remember you
heard it here first.
Elinor Outside an amusement arcade—in a shopping "mall". (*She laughs*)
It is a repulsive word, I'm right. (*She paces, smoking, her mood darkening*)
I will *not* have him interfering in my arrangements, Christopher, under any
circumstances.
Christopher Forget about Al. (*Gently*) Think how hard he has to run just to
keep up, in any way at all.

Elinor paces, then she laughs

Elinor Yes, well, it's the last time he takes me out for a night on the town!

Black-out

SCENE 4

Al is alone on stage with the next airtight bag

Al I still wake up in a sweat sometimes thinking about that night! I did *not*
take her out to work on her at all. (*He moves, stops, and smiles*) Well,
maybe ten per cent. (*He peers close into the bag*) So we come to what
should be one of the most momentous bags of all. (*He opens it*) But in fact
there is only a half-empty tin of barley sugars, and a fragment of a child's
picture. (*He stares at the fragment*) This was huge once.

Joanna enters, scantily clad in summer clothes

There were tiny hints that something was about to break…

*Joanna stands against the wall. He comes up to her, kissing her on the
shoulder, holding some papers in one hand, Joanna in the other. Al turns
back to us*

When it happened I was deep in paperwork, naturally. (*He turns back to
Joanna, about to kiss her, then looks up*) I wish I had been able to keep
Barbara's sneakers—I will always connect that moment with her new
incredibly clean sneakers!

Barbara comes running on, wearing crisp wonderfully clean sneakers

Barbara Have you heard?
Al (*moving a respectable distance from Joanna*) Heard what?
Barbara You haven't heard!
Al No. What is it?
Barbara I thought Christopher was coming here to tell you. You really haven't heard?
Al No, we can do this all afternoon, if you like. (*Patiently*) What is it?
Barbara (*excited*) If you haven't heard, I don't think I can tell you yet. (*She pauses slightly*) Afraid not!

Barbara exits

Joanna What on earth is going on?
Al I think we are about to find out.

Barbara enters

Barbara I've got to tell you! I can't stop myself, he's done it, he's made it work. (*She pauses slightly*) He's done the Sun Battery!

Silence

Al No!
Barbara He has. The Sun Battery!
Al Jesus, I'm stunned.

Momentary pause

I didn't know he was near something that big.
Barbara Yes! I've got to get back, isn't it wonderful? (*She moves*) He's almost ready to show you—you'll be called.

Barbara exits

Joanna That sounds promising, I like the name—the Sun Battery? How important is it?
Al (*slowly*) We've got to remember everything about today. What the weather was like, what we're wearing.
Joanna (*startled, laughing*) It's *that* important?
Al Important? (*Exuberant*) It's fucking incredible! It's amazing. (*He moves, pacing, thinking*) I knew he had an interest in the Sun Battery ... but his main work is different. He must have been doing this on the side. (*He looks up*) It's magnificent! (*He moves towards Joanna*) Of course, when you see

it, *if* you see it, the enormity of it all will not be obvious. It'll just look like a tedious little tube.

Joanna (*with an excited laugh*) A tedious tube!

Al Yes—with minute bubbles. (*He laughs and moves*) You see, Joanna, you visit a sleepy science department, with all those funny smells you haven't known since school, and look what happens! You witness this!

Joanna (*loudly*) Al! For Chrissake, Al! Explain it to me. In words of not more than one syllable. Make me understand.

Slight pause

Al It's easy to keep it simple—fossil fuel is going to run out, right?

Joanna (*laughing*) I can understand *that*.

Al There is an almost unlimited supply of water——

Joanna I can understand that too!

Al Water contains hydrogen. But how to get it out? Some chemical reactions are caused by shining a light. Find the right chemical to act as a catalyst—shine a light, a beam, above all, the sun—and you can create hydrogen out of sunlight and water. Hydrogen, which can run planes, cars, anything you want. And when you burn it, it will turn back to water. Polluting nothing. People have been trying to do it for years.

Silence

Joanna (*with an excited laugh*) I'll remember what I'm wearing!

Muzak

Barbara supervises as the equipment is brought in. A simple wooden table, completely bare, except for a metal stand and clamp holding a glass tube

The muzak really swells up. It is coming from elsewhere in the building, a radio blaring out light orchestral music. A beam of light stabs across the darkened stage. The tube starts bubbling

Al, Elinor, Joanna and Christopher stand waiting. Barbara a little apart

Al This music is so inappropriate. It is the cleaners in the passage. Shall I...?

Christopher (*gently cutting him off*) Don't worry about the music, Al.

Out of respect, Al lets Elinor move forward first. Elinor approaches the table, she stands alone in the beam of light, staring down at the apparatus. She takes out a tin of barley sugars from her pocket, all the time staring. She slips a barley sugar into her mouth

Elinor? Do you see it?

Elinor Oh yes. Absolutely ... this is good. (*Very respectfully*) Is it based on titanium dioxide? No, no, I know nothing can be declared until the patent is through; the catalyst. (*She muses to herself, quietly excited*) Is it anatase or rutile? You haven't used an absorbed dye to shift the Lambda-max, clearly——

Christopher The particles have an electrodeposited coating. It's only a few nanometres thick so refractive-index matching makes it——

Elinor Yes, it certainly seems to have a high quantum yield. Maybe there's an added sulfonated surfactant to enhance mass transport at the surface?

Christopher No. (*Smiling warmly*) Think more a photocatalytic system——

Joanna (*with an excited smile*) I can't understand any of that! But I saw the light hit the water and it made it happen. It's great to be one of the first in the world to see it. I'm getting goosebumps.

Al (*quietly*) It does work, Christopher ... it's beautiful.

Elinor suddenly moves over to Christopher and gives him a little kiss

Elinor Well done. (*Very crisply*) I didn't think this would happen in my lifetime. Thank you for showing it to me.

Pause

Super.

Elinor exits

Barbara (*sharply*) Is that all? Doesn't she want to see it again?

Christopher She's pleased. That is Elinor being over the moon.

Al I know it's an obvious thing to say but I'm going to say it—I'm proud to be here!

Christopher I thought for one moment you were lost for words.

Barbara (*to Al*) Do *you* want to see any more?

Al No. (*Suddenly*) I want to be alone with Christopher, now. Please, quickly. If you could ... sorry to bundle you out—we must be *alone*.

Joanna and Barbara exit

The Lights switch back on. Christopher and Al are alone on stage

You bastard! You've done it!

Christopher Yes.

Al It's fantastic news.

Christopher That's right.

Al I think I always knew! I knew you'd do something big. And Elinor—just now ... watching it, so still, but so excited... (*He paces*) I hear on the grapevine Utah were making progress ... but four years away probably, at least.

Christopher I heard that.

Al Imagine what they'll feel like when they know! (*Gleefully*) It's fucking great! (*He turns*) Is the catalyst coated rutile? (*He laughs*) Just a guess. What is it?

Christopher (*calmly*) Not yet, Al. Not till the patent's through.

Al Not even me? (*With a quick glance*) OK! I don't need to know till the right time. (*He walks excitedly*) Let us compute what it means—the department is secure, obviously! *For the rest of time.* Millions will be coming in here. (*He grins*) Millions for you too, of course. The Nobel Prize, naturally.

Christopher (*calmly*) Come on, Al, it may not be that big. It's got to be proven to be economic.

Al I'm allowed to do this today of all days! That's what I'm here for. (*He looks across at Christopher*) What a feeling it must be knowing you're getting nearer and nearer to something all the time—and only you and your research team know anything about it. What does that really feel like?

Christopher (*grinning*) Oh, Al!

Al Don't say it.

Christopher What was I going to say?

Al That I think like a tabloid.

Christopher But you do. (*He smiles affectionately*) And that's what's great about you. You're right, I'll have to know how I'm going to answer *that* question.

Al When are you going to publish?

Christopher I'm going to make a straight announcement first.

Al turns

That we've achieved it.

Al is very startled. Silence

Al What? *Before* you've published?

Christopher Yes.

Al (*urgently*) Is that wise?

Christopher (*calmly*) Of course. Otherwise it'll leak out. I'll invite Briskin and Moiseiwitsch over from Oxford, to inspect it, as a precaution. And then I will announce it immediately to the world press. (*He looks straight at Al*) *When* the patent is through, I will publish.

Al Christopher ... don't you think you should wait till then? And let others repeat the experiment?
Christopher What is this, Al? I've done it, for Chrissake. Why the caution? I *owe* it to the university, to show we're first.

Silence

Al What do I know? I'm sorry.

Christopher moves

Christopher You've helped, you know, Al.
Al (*lightly*) Now that's a lie, quite clearly.
Christopher (*benignly*) No, you've helped—by just being there.

Christopher exits

Al is by himself

The apparatus is moved off and a rolled-up picture is placed on one of the bench seats

The Lighting turns to strong sunlight

Al So now we come to the child's picture. (*He moves over to the bench seats, to the rolled-up picture. He switches the tannoy on*)

A buzz of expectant chattering voices comes out of the tannoy, gradually building louder and louder, pouring out towards Al. The sound of people waiting for a press conference

As Al listens, the service area of a cafeteria comes on. Charlie, a man in his late fifties, is standing behind the metal service units

There is one table with upturned chairs on it, placed the other side of the stage

(*Listening to the voices*) The hacks gather, Charlie ... even the weather is in sympathy. This is a terrific heatwave.
Charlie Wonderful day, sir. In every sense.

Christopher's voice comes, popping the microphone

Christopher (*over tannoy*) Gentlemen, gentlemen, please, I think we are just about ready to begin. I will read the statement and then you can ask questions. I have an announcement to make——

Al reaches up and switches the tannoy off. Silence. Al's manner is very preoccupied

Charlie You're not going in there?
Al Not yet, no.
Charlie Prefer to keep out of the way, sir? Listen to it among the mushy peas?
Al I *am* going to go in there and listen—in a moment.
Charlie It's one of the best times I can remember in the thirty-five years I've been here. The old sense of excitement is back. And didn't we need it! People look happier, even when eating this food!

Pause

Al (*quietly*) We did need it, yes, Charlie.
Charlie There's a real sense of going forward again, isn't there, sir? I could always tell when something was up with the scientists in the old days, because they'd come rushing in here with absolute ferocious appetites, just a few *seconds* before we closed.

Al moves around, in thought

I've seen all the greats we've had here, sir, and as soon as I got to know Dr Christopher, I knew he was—most likely—one of them.
Al (*quietly*) Those have been my feelings, too, Charlie. (*He looks up*) Sorry—you want to listen? (*Suddenly*) Why don't *you* go in there, it's OK. Go on, I'll guard the cafeteria.
Charlie Can I, sir? Good. It is something not to be missed, isn't it!

Charlie exits

Al moves round the cafeteria, preoccupied

Ghislane enters, a striking-looking woman, beautifully dressed

Al Ghislane! What are you doing? Why aren't you in there?
Ghislane (*with an excited smile*) Just came out for a breath of fresh air. The journalists are sweating so much! (*She looks across*) Why are *you* here?
Al Press conferences make me nervous. Not that I've ever been to one before. (*He smiles*) This one is making me nervous.
Ghislane (*laughing*) Me too! Do you think Christopher's doing it right? Is he talking too fast? Have you managed to hear any of it, Al?

Al He's doing fine. (*He smiles*) And you look fabulous, as always.
Ghislane (*warmly, excited*) Thank you, Al. *You* look just the same.
Al You mean despite being a professor! (*He indicates the tannoy*) Your whole life is changing in there…
Ghislane (*laughing nervously*) No, no, don't say that!
Al (*pleasantly*) Oh, yes, you'll have to start practising law in America, because that's where you'll be. A big house! Celebrity! Christopher becoming a household name—as near as a scientist can come to one!
Ghislane I don't want that for him. *Celebrity.* It's just good to know after all the incredible long hours he's done, it's all been worthwhile.

Al watches her in the strong sunlight

Al He need never do anything ever again, Ghislane, you realize.
Ghislane Well, of course he will. He must. But to wake up every morning, knowing what you've achieved … whatever happens now! You've done one of the most important things for … for goodness knows how long, by the time you're forty-one! (*She is really excited*) That must be amazing, knowing that, feeling that. (*She turns*) It's bloody great, Al, isn't it?
Al Yes. (*Lightly*) Not to mention the money, the books, the movie.

Ghislane laughs

You can negotiate the rights yourself.
Ghislane (*laughing*) Stop it, Al, *please!* (*She moves*) You've always thought that Chris had it in him, to do something special, haven't you?
Al (*thoughtfully*) Yes, I did.

Ghislane doesn't notice his pensive mood

Ghislane So have I! (*She moves around*) And I've always loved him more than I can say. It seems the morning to say it. However obvious it might be! (*She indicates the tannoy*) Turn him up, Al, for Chrissake, I want to hear—we're missing it!

Al turns the volume up. We hear questions being fired at Christopher, over the tannoy

Reporter (*over tannoy*) Where were you born?
Christopher (*over tannoy*) A little unromantic village called Reddington in Shropshire.
Reporter (*over tannoy*) How old are you?
Christopher (*over tannoy*) Getting personal. I'm thirty-eight years old.

Ghislane starts slightly, glances round at Al

Al Really? So he's thirty-eight now.

Ghislane (*reaching up, turning the tannoy off*) A little embroidery! Very wicked. Oh, Christopher...! (*She laughs*) He doesn't want to reach forty.

Al Knocked three years off. If this goes on—he'll be twenty-five by tea time.

Ghislane (*laughing it off*) I'm sure you've done it, Al! Doesn't everybody do it?

Al (*after a very slight pause*) Yes, of course.

Elinor enters, Joanna just behind. Elinor's mood is very up

Elinor So *this* is where you are.

Al We just popped out for a moment.

Elinor Yes. Well, the questions have got stupid now, it's time for a break. (*She laughs*) Did you hear him lying about his age? The vanity of men! Really!

Joanna He did it very confidently too. (*She mimes*) "I'm *thirty-eight* years old."

Elinor But he's handling it jolly well—I think they realize how important it is.

Al They must—even my seven-year-old daughter does! I've brought along a picture she's done, to show Christopher. It's on rather an epic scale. (*He holds the picture up. It show a battery, like a colossal domestic torch battery, warming up the world, with the sun coming out of it*) This is the rain forest ... and all the animals, being rescued by Christopher's non-polluting battery. Not very scientifically accurate—but you see it appeals even to the very young.

Elinor (*staring at the picture for a second*) Very striking, Albie! (*Teasingly*) She's inherited your——

Al (*simultaneously*) My artistic talent. That's right!

Ghislane It's touching. You *must* show it to Christopher.

Elinor If he ever gets away from all the TV crews treading on each other. It's rather different from when——

Al (*quickly*) You announced the discovery of the structure of vitamins.

Elinor Yes. (*With a self-mocking laugh*) But then of course we did it how it should be done—old George and I were photographed just for the *local paper*.

Al Didn't stop him trying to grab all the credit though...!

Elinor Now, now...

Al (*grinning*) She despises anything commercial.

Elinor Of course.

Ghislane But a little hype is permissible—isn't it, Elinor?

Elinor Today, yes, because it's justified. (*She moves across the cafeteria*)
No doubt soon, there will be science Oscars—nominations for the best new
treatment for stomach ulcers, or the best supporting Alternative Energy
Oscar.
Al Why not? That's right! "Best detector for explosives in an urban
situation"! (*He begins to write in a notebook*)
Elinor Oh, Albie, what are you doing? Not making notes today.
Al Just one ... "The Science Oscars".

Ghislane turns up the tannoy. The sound of people beginning to move

Christopher (*over tannoy*) Now, gentlemen, I would like you to accompany
me to the laboratory.
Ghislane They've finished. Great! It's all done. (*She turns the tannoy off*)
Al Yes—the story's about to go round the world. There's no going back now.
Ghislane Al, stop it! He thinks our lives are changing for ever. (*With an
excited laugh*) Well, *maybe they are*! And maybe that's good. (*She moves*)
Let's get in there! Come on, everybody.
Elinor Yes, super. I'm coming. (*She moves to exit*) You too, Albie, come on.
Al Yes, I'm coming. (*He watches her go, but he doesn't move*)

Elinor exits

Joanna You've put your daughter's picture away. Why? I thought you were
going to show it to Christopher...

Silence

Al, what's troubling you?
Al Who said anything was troubling me?
Joanna Don't play for time, what is it?

Pause

Al I can't work out how he has done it.
Joanna So—is that such a surprise?
Al (*lightly*) You mean because it's *me*—that means nothing? That's
probably right. (*More seriously*) But I've been reading what he's let me
see. Even allowing for the fact he's keeping something back ... it's... (*He
pauses*) It's a little cloudy... (*He moves*)
Joanna But you've seen it work. The demonstration—*you've seen it*.
Al Of course. I have, yes. So it must be true. (*Loudly*) I want Christopher to
be right, for God's sake—I want this to be a wonderful day. I really do! (*He
pauses*) It's only—I can't see how he's done it.

Silence

Joanna (*whistling*) If it was a fake—Jesus! A *fraud*…
Al That is certainly not what has happened. That word must not be used.
Joanna It'd be amazing, though, if it was happening—what a story.
Al No. No, Joanna. More information … I'm sure that's all it needs, to
squeeze a little more information out of him, somehow.

Black-out

SCENE 5

Al is c. He takes off his jacket, and moves forward in his shirt sleeves

Al Things become nocturnal now. (*He holds up the fifth plastic bag*) A tin
of baking powder, Sainsbury's Baking Powder. (*He stares at it for a
moment with fascination*) It would be fair to say this is one of the more
important tins of my life. (*He moves forward and pulls up the floor*)

*The middle of the stage opens like a flower. A dark recess, like a large grave,
is revealed*

As well as nocturnal, we get a little subterranean. (*He climbs down into the
recess*)

Joanna enters, and stands on the edge of the hole, staring down

*Al begins to throw strangely-shaped objects out of the hole, fragments of
broken scientific equipment, old jars of chemicals, both large and small, an
extraordinary time warp of scientific detritus, many of the objects jagged and
surreal. Music, some Bach, is drifting from somewhere deep in the building*

Joanna Careful!

Al throws up another object. It spins across the floor towards her

Careful! Jesus, Al—what *are those*?
Al That's some tellurium bromide, from the early fifties, it looks like. Around
the day I was born! And here is some ferro-cyanide, even older, from the
forties——
Joanna (*jumping out of the way*) Cyanide! It's not leaking—not going to
leak, Al?

Al Don't worry. (*He grins*) Just don't lick it.

Al comes out of the hole, and sits on the side, holding a sinister and mangled piece of darkened metal

Joanna And what is that horrible-looking thing?
Al This, believe it or not, is something very innocent, charming even.
Joanna Charming?

Al stares at the fragment for a moment

Al Yes... You'll never guess what this once was... It is part of a very old computer terminal. Imagine how thrilled they were when this first worked. The joy... (*He holds it up to his ear like a sea shell*) Can you hear the future?
Joanna (*taking it and gently holding it up to her ear*) Or the past....
Al (*grinning*) People over the years whenever they finished with anything, they must have chucked it down here, didn't matter how dangerous. Just happily tossed it into this place. (*He picks up another strange fragment. More intensely*) Amazing, the merry incompetence that went on, isn't it? (*He stares down at the fragment*) When they were giddy with the possibilities of everything.

Pause

Joanna That's quite serious—for you, Al!
Al (*with another object*) This is beautiful, though—an ancient Kipps.
Joanna Where's that music coming from?
Al That's Elinor's music. She always has it on when she's working. If you can hear it, you know she's in her lab. (*He pulls out another metal object*)
Joanna That's really gross, Al, that one! I don't know what you're doing this sleuthing for anyway? What you expecting to find, that Christopher did something *here*?
Al I'm not expecting to find anything. My doubts are almost certainly groundless... Just keeps me away from more admin!
Joanna And what am I doing here?
Al (*with an unabashed smile*) You just can't stop coming back for more
Joanna Really! (*With a warm laugh*) Patronising bastard!
Al (*touching her*) You are quite properly intrigued by the situation...

He takes her arm, lifts her down into the dark recess

Joanna Not here, Al, for Chrissake, it's dangerous.
Al (*grinning*) Not while you're with me.

Joanna You're sure? *Shit*! I'm touching something.
Al (*touching her breasts*) That's some hexa-fluoro-something…

She laughs

I never expected to find old chemistry sexy!

Elinor enters

Elinor Albie! I might have known it was you.

Al uncoils himself from around Joanna

Al Elinor! Your music's playing—you should still be in your lab.
Elinor (*staring down at him in the hole*) I was taking a short break, when I
heard some rather strange noises.
Al Well, I was just… (*He indicates Joanna*) Well, you could see part of what
I was just doing.
Elinor Yes. And what was the other part?
Al The other part? I, I, I was just checking there's nothing dangerous amongst
all the junk that's been dumped here. (*He produces another strange
fragment of old equipment, out of the floor*)

Elinor is in a warm, exuberant mood

Elinor The Professor of the Department needs to do that!
Al Why not? I am a compulsive cleaner-upper. I used to ask to stay behind
at school, so I could pick up the lost property.
Joanna You would have!
Elinor (*lightly*) I don't believe that's all you're doing here, Albie.
Al Well, what do you think I'm doing? Keeping an eye on you? (*To Joanna*)
Elinor never goes home, or more accurately, she's never *seen* to go home.

*Elinor moves among the objects that are strewn across the stage, inspecting
them*

Elinor Well, there are advantages to being single.
Joanna A real obsessive scientist.
Elinor I hope not! On the surface maybe. (*She laughs*) I suppose I am usually
either in the lab, or else stalking the passages.
Al (*suddenly daring to tease her*) She passes by—humming Bach!
Elinor Yes, well, I try to blot out all external noise with the music in my lab.
Every now and then I stop it—and have a listen to the outside world, to
check what's going on. (*She laughs*) And I'm not missing much!

Al (*grinning*) You're what Joanna thought all scientists were like—until she met me, that is.

Elinor (*straight at him*) Yes, that must have been a shock—clearly, Albie— meeting you. (*She moves across the debris, examining pieces with curiosity*) For some reason people still think of scientists as either evil geniuses who are totally oblivious to the effect of their work—good Lord, this Kipps must be at least fifty years old—don't they? (*She picks up another object*) Or else saintly boffins who are actually born wearing their white coats.

Joanna And what category do you fit in?

Elinor Do I *have* to be in a category?

Al Ask her what work she's doing...

Joanna (*laughing*) What work are you doing?

Elinor Well, part of that is confidential.

Al (*loudly*) You see, she's secretive as well!

Elinor I'm only partly secretive!

Al Makes all the difference. (*Teasingly, warmly*) She doesn't have to dirty herself with raising sponsorship—has funding for life from the university. She needn't ever even whisper anything about her work, until *she* wants to.

Elinor Yes—and it's wonderful.

Al (*teasing, but very loud, intense*) Tell what it is. The work. It's only us here. Come on, tell me, tell me now. *Tell me*!

Elinor No, Albie. No, no, *no*.

Al Tell!

Elinor (*bellowing*) NO!

They face each other

That should be fairly clear—even to you, Albie.

Al opens his mouth to speak

And don't you dare try asking again!

Al She's so strict!

Silence

Elinor When I'm ready, and not before. (*She smiles*) You will be *among* the first to know.

Al Will I? (*Lightly*) I'll try to be patient. (*He opens a panel in the side of the stage, to reveal a cluster of more objects, spooky old canisters, large metal fragments, piles of yellowing papers stuffed into the skirting of the building*)

Elinor What have you found now? You'll produce a corpse next. (*She moves*) Just think, with this breakthrough we will be able to rip all these passages out anyway! Rebuild—I might even get an extra room.
Al Of course. A whole new floor, Elinor—a wing if necessary.
Elinor (*with a warm laugh*) Well, that might be a trifle excessive, Albie, a floor will do! Maybe a private bathroom ... a jacuzzi or two.
Al (*quickly*) So you don't object to profiting from the commercial exploitation of Christopher's work, then?
Elinor Don't be silly, I'm not *that* much of a puritan. (*She laughs*) You think I'm daft! I will tuck into what we're going to get, just like everyone else. (*She stops, stares across at them*) It's a splendid time. (*She turns, more brisk again, moving to exit*) You'll put all this back, won't you? And a safety officer should be called the very first thing in the morning. (*She moves*) And don't forget to switch off the lights.

Elinor exits

Al (*watching her go*) Yes, Elinor...

Pause

I've never dared to talk to her like that before ... she was really happy tonight, so I got away with it. (*He moves*) Sometimes, she still treats me as if I'm nineteen...
Joanna Sometimes I think you're in love with her.

Al turns and smiles

Al I admire her, certainly.
Joanna More.
Al (*reflecting on her words*) You think? I'm fascinated by her, I admit. The way she speaks, her "supers", her barley sugars, her arrogance, her scrupulousness, her ability ... her smell even.
Joanna Her smell?
Al *Yes*—you're transported straight back to the fifties. It's almost as if she's bottled it ... like the leather seats of a classic car. It's addictive. (*He moves*) I can remember those smells from my childhood. (*He looks up*) She wears scent in the lab! It's wonderful... (*He stares in the direction of her music*) But she's still a real force, of course ... still a great lady. (*He pauses*) Soon we'll see the fruits of all that work... (*He starts putting the objects back into the hole. The more fragile glass ones he replaces gently, the metal objects he kicks*)
Joanna (*keeping out of the way of flying metal objects*) Mind! (*She stares*

down into the hole) It's really strange to see among all these old chemicals—
a tin of baking powder.
Al Baking powder? (*Louder*) Where's the baking powder?
Joanna (*with a startled laugh, mimicking him*) "Where's the baking
powder"? There! (*She points in the hole*) And some bleach... What's the
matter?

Al leaps down into the hole

Al Bleach! Oh, shit, yes!
Joanna What's the matter, Al? Why's that bad? Tell me—I hate not
understanding.

Al sits on the corner of the hole, with the tin of baking powder

Silence

Al This will sound mad—but one of the ways of faking the Sun Battery ...
would be to use baking powder and bleach—with calcium hydride you
could fake the whole thing.
Joanna Oh, come on! Christopher used baking powder! You really can't be
serious ... can you?
Al (*quietly*) I'm seldom serious, I know...

Pause

But I don't like finding it.
Joanna Distinguished scientists have seen the demonstration.
Al Never means anything. They saw what they were shown. (*He moves*)
Conjurers always say the best audiences for magic tricks—the most
gullible—are scientists. They believe what they see. (*He turns*) He hasn't
published yet, has he?
Joanna But he can't have used something as simple as that. This is
Christopher...! It *can't* be that crude.
Al Why not? Most notorious scientific frauds *have* been very crude. That's
what's so interesting. They're sometimes startlingly blatant—people
colouring mice for instance with black felt tip pens. Good scientists!

Pause

Joanna is among the debris

Joanna But I mean, he wouldn't drop the evidence in here—*preserving* it,
for you to poke around and find. He'd destroy it.

Al I'm not sure you're right about that. In a funny way this is where I'd put it too, among the other scientific equipment. That way you're not admitting anything, even to yourself.

Joanna (*seriously, louder*) Al—you don't *really* believe he's faked it, do you?

Al (*loudly, urgently*) I don't know! I really don't.

Silence. He moves

But any doubts are serious. (*He paces among the debris*) This is the one area of human activity where cheating still matters! It means your career is switched off. (*He flicks his fingers sharply*) Just like that. (*He stops pacing*) The thoughts are ridiculous—they must be—but they keep coming back... (*He pushes the debris violently back into the hole*)

Black-out

SCENE 6

Al is standing US *by the lockers*

Al So where is it? The one with the deadly yellow notebook. (*He rips open the sixth bag, and stares inside*) What on earth are these? Oh yes, a clump of ear plugs, at least I think that's what they once were, they've changed colour. A truly repulsive exhibit, I admit ... but it's difficult to keep mementoes of lack of sleep.

Early morning light comes up

The Professor comes on and stands next to Al

Professor I thought I didn't have to come to meetings this early any more, it better be important, Albert.

Al Well, in a way I really hope it isn't. *First*, I want to say about Christopher——

Professor There is no need for a preamble—come to the point.

Al Well, with respect I think I *do* need to say this. As you know, I admire Christopher greatly—we both know how good he is.

Professor A mistake. Never admire anyone.

Al What? That's a very bleak attitude.

Professor Of course. But they only disappoint. They *always* disappoint. I have never met anybody I've considered worthy of admiration—once I've

got to know them. (*He turns suddenly*) So, Albert, you think something's
wrong with the Sun Battery?

Al (*after a slight pause, startled*) Yes. Possibly. I think there is a *chance* the
results are suspect.

Professor He faked them?

Al If you must.

Professor What do you mean, if I must? What you're saying is—he's faked
them.

Al I *might* be saying that. Have you a view on the work? What do you think?

Professor We are not here to discuss what I think, thank God. On the face
of it, what he's shown me, is plausible——

Al (*relieved*) Good! You're right, of course. I should forget my doubts.

Professor Did I say that?

Al No, but I'm hoping you're saying that. I have no evidence, baking powder,
his restlessness about being here, it's nothing! I have no desire at all to harm
his reputation.

Professor You shouldn't worry about that.

Al Why ever not?

Professor Because you have to protect the department.

Al *I* have—just *me*?

Professor A fraud would be *appalling*, naturally. (*He pauses*) But you can
negotiate with him.

Al (*surprised*) Negotiate? How do I do that?

Professor Let him know you may have doubts. If they are founded in any
way, you can negotiate a retraction, "the result's no longer conclusive",
etc. etc. But if you are right, he *must* retract. You cannot just wait and see.

Al (*exasperated*) I can't deal with this! He's a close friend—what do I say
to him? "Excuse me, Chris, have you perpetrated one of the biggest
scientific frauds of the last fifty years…? Oh, really, you might have? Fine!
Let's negotiate!"

Pause

And please don't tell me I'm Head of the Department!

Professor But you are, Albert. (*Smoothly*) And in fact, news of your
organizational skills have begun to spread beyond these walls—how
you've re-planned the department, stopped the rot here.

Al (*dismissively*) Oh, really… (*He moves*) I've just had a brilliant idea, why
don't you come back? Become an *active* Emeritus?

Professor That is clearly impossible. (*He pauses*) Does anybody else know
about this?

Al No. Except Elinor. I sent her a short note, which I rewrote many times.

Professor It is not Elinor's responsibility.

Al I know. But she is always a help to me.

Professor She won't be. (*He looks at Al*) It is a difficult situation, Albert, I realize, but actually I think you're rather better qualified to deal with it than most.

Al Oh, really? In what way?

Professor You have a curiosity about people, which I for one, completely lack.

Al rolls his eyes

I cannot deal with their messiness, their contradictions, but I think you enjoy all that. And unlike me, you are not a jealous person. I'm afraid I have always been surprisingly jealous of my colleagues. Elinor ... many others... (*He moves to exit*) Since you ask my advice, Albert, I'll give you some. Hesitate and you might be finished, on the other hand, do something and you may prosper.

Professor exits

Al Thanks! Great! (*He stares after him*) Evil old sod!

The Lights get brighter. Al sits at his large desk. There is the sound of birdsong. People's radios in the distance. Al is on the phone

(*Into the phone*) Hallo, honey ... yes, it's me, Daddy. ... I missed my usual time to see you, I know. The first time ever, isn't it, yes? ... But I've been up all night in my office. ... (*Lightly*) Well, you know your dad people leave him to arrange things. ... I'll be there next week, I promise. ... You've done another picture, of the Sun Battery? Is it as big as the other one? ... Bigger!

Barbara comes bursting in, laden with baskets of food

(*Into the phone*) I'll see you, honey. (*He rings off, and looks up*) Barbara! Good Lord, what's all that for?

Barbara It's the picnic! You haven't forgotten, have you?

Al The picnic? Oh, no, no.

Barbara We're all bringing things for it. Haven't you got something?

Al Yes, yes, of course—somewhere. I think I brought a couple of tins of corned beef.

Barbara You certainly splashed out, didn't you!

Al Well— (*with a mocking smile*) since it's a time of celebration, I thought I would. (*He stares at her*)

Barbara You wanted to see me?
Al Yes.
Barbara Here I am, then.

Their eyes meet

Al Yes… (*Awkwardly*) Have you been enjoying the last few weeks, Barbara?
Barbara Of course, it's been the most exciting time of my life.
Al Are you sure?
Barbara Am I sure? What do you mean by that?
Al (*moving rather groggily*) I know the tins of corned beef are somewhere— lack of sleep does funny things, forgive me. (*Casually*) So you're not troubled by anything?
Barbara (*with a hard look*) What sort of things did you have in mind?
Al I think you know what I mean.

Barbara looks at him blankly

Irregularities with the work?
Barbara No.
Al No? Just like that? (*He looks at her*) No.
Barbara *No.*

Pause

Al (*looking for tins*) I don't really think making a solemn appeal to your duty as a scientist will work with you, Barbara——
Barbara But you're going to do it anyway.
Al I'll just point out, you've been working very closely with Christopher. It's natural for you to blot things out, that you might have seen, that don't quite … fit. (*He looks at her*) When you came running in to tell the news in your new sneakers, that morning, so excited! Was that tinged with anything? Any doubts? Were you thinking—if I shout loud enough, it will make it true?
Barbara We were *all* excited that day, I seem to remember.

Pause

Al Yes. (*Softly*) You are very able, Barbara, I know that, ambitious, in a good way. If there is to be any unpleasantness——
Barbara (*sharply*) Unpleasantness?
Al There is no need for you to be involved. Your career could quite easily be unscathed if——

Barbara That's not very subtle.
Al (*suddenly*) I've never done this before—I don't know how to do it subtly!
Jesus! Can one do this kind of thing subtly?
Barbara And I've hardly got much of a career to scathe.
Al You will have. (*He pauses*) So?

Very slight pause

Barbara There is nothing to tell.
Al (*exasperated, loudly*) I need to know the truth, Barbara—I don't care what
it is, as long as I know!

We hear the sound of Christopher and Ghislane laughing, approaching

Barbara You must ask Christopher. It is his work.
Al Of course. Is that all, Barbara?
Barbara Yes. (*She gets up*) Yes. (*She moves her baskets of food*) I have a
little yellow notebook, with a rose on the front. It looks like a child's diary.
Al (*impatiently*) Yes.
Barbara I made a few notes of my own. (*Slowly*) I'll go over those again,
just in case. (*Pointedly*) I will re-read them in the light of what you've said.

Christopher and Ghislane enter, carrying baskets groaning with food

Christopher You don't look as if you're ready!
Ghislane You *haven't* forgotten, Al, have you?
Al No, no, no.

He stares at them as they put down the picnic baskets

(*Genuinely warm*) You look wonderful, you two. Great. As always.
Christopher We thought we'd really overdo it, because we don't know
when we'll all be doing this again.
Ghislane We've got a lot of really strong cheeses, champagne, of course,
smoked fish, smoked eel even. We could hardly move the bicycles!
Christopher There's enough food here even for you, Al.
Ghislane And hats! Of course! So we could really be like one of those
vintage picnics.
Barbara A boffins' picnic.
Al Yes—I have a tin of spam somewhere. No, no, I malign myself, two tins
of corned beef.
Christopher (*laughing*) Al, we're honoured.
Al Yes. (*He moves*) I need to have a word with Christopher.

Christopher (*very elated*) Fine. What is it?

Al No, I need to make a time, an appointment with you.

Christopher An appointment? That's very formal. It might be a little difficult, because we're going to the States first thing in the morning.

Al What, so soon? For how long?

Ghislane A couple of months. There's so much interest in him, he's going initially just for some exploratory talks.

Barbara gathers the bags

Barbara (*to Ghislane*) I'll help you get these things into the car, while they talk. I can smell the cheeses, from here, they'll probably set alarms off, they're so strong.

Ghislane (*surprised*) Right. OK. (*She laughs*) If we must! (*She picks up some bags*) Don't you dare keep him long, Al, please!

Barbara and Ghislane exit

Al They've forgotten the fruit. (*He stares after them*) There's never any time now, is there?

Christopher (*breezily*) There was never any time, with us, not really. Always been too busy. (*He looks at Al*) What is it, Al?

Al (*taking a deep breath*) Being busy ... that touches on what I wanted to say. (*He moves*) Since you made your announcement to the press, everything has gone at such a speed——

Christopher (*smiling at this*) Yes?

Al You don't ... you don't think anything could have been overlooked?

Christopher What do you think I've overlooked, Al?

Al I don't *think* you've overlooked anything, I just want to know if there's the slightest possibility that something might have been missed.

Christopher You'll have to be more specific.

Slight pause

Al (*swallowing*) I mean ... there aren't any inconsistencies ... anything that could have been *fudged*?

Christopher Fudged...? (*With a spontaneous laugh*) You're not suggesting I've been cheating, Al?

Al seems stranded c

Al I ... no ... I...

Christopher (*with a warm laugh*) You are! Aren't you? Almost! (*He smiles, relaxed*) You little fucker.

Al No, no, I just want to be sure. (*He looks straight at him*) This little fucker just wants to be absolutely sure.

Christopher (*relaxed*) You really think I would fudge results, risk everything, when it could be disproved in ten minutes. It makes no sense at all.

Al (*with a nervous laugh*) You would have to be crazy, I know!

Christopher What is this, Al? You don't want it to be happening?

Al Of course I want it to be successful—more than anything.

Christopher (*softly*) Yes. I think you do.

Al (*urgently*) There just mustn't be any little kinks we don't know about.

Christopher I promise you, Al—listen to this—everything is fine, everything has been achieved. *There are no kinks.*

Al (*quickly*) Nothing Barbara or anybody else might have done for demonstration purposes ... to help along just one demonstration. (*He nervously pulls at the bag of grapes*)

Christopher (*very firmly*) Al—there's absolutely nothing that can be produced to shake the results in any way. Nothing—not even in a plastic bag.

Silence

Al Right, of course, I'm sorry to have mentioned anything.

Christopher (*nonchalantly*) No, no, you had to probe. You were doing your job. I understand.

Ghislane and Barbara enter

Ghislane Look at them, they've started eating the food! Al, you're eating the picnic.

Al Am I? Oh, yes.

Barbara He forgot to bring his share—and now he's eating the rest!

Christopher (*grinning*) He's been interrogating me—that always makes people hungry.

Ghislane Interrogating you, today ... what on earth for?

Al I just needed reassurance.

Barbara (*watchful, sharply*) And did you get it?

Christopher Yes. At least I hope he did. (*He looks at him. Fondly*) You mustn't worry, Al—these are great days.

Al Yes, I know—great days.

Elinor and Joanna enter, all dressed up

Elinor Are we late? I hope we're not late.

Joanna (*staring at Al's crumpled appearance*) Looking at Al—I don't think we can be.

Al (*startled*) Why's everybody dressed up? It's only a picnic!

Elinor But it's a celebration too—it's important to do these things properly.

Al (*close to her, private*) Elinor, can I...?

Elinor (*seemingly not hearing, indicating Christopher*) It's the least he deserves!

Joanna (*to Al*) And I hope it's the day you decide we are going on holiday together.

Al tries to get Elinor's attention, he glances at Joanna

Al You and me? Together? (*After a slight pause*) Of course. (*Directly, urgently*) Elinor?

There is the sound of people playing computer games in nearby rooms. Elinor is standing with her back to Al

Christopher Come on, everybody, let's get out of here before the weather changes! Barbara, have you got the camera, have you remembered?

Barbara Oh, yes, I'm going to be official photographer. There're going to be some great pictures——

Ghislane Of this historic feast.

Barbara exits

Elinor (*moving*) I think I might even allow myself to catch some sun today. (*She laughs*) My skin will have the shock of its life! Albie! Ready?

Al Nearly ... I'm still looking for my contribution.

Ghislane (*laughing*) Oh, Al—you're incorrigible.

Christopher and Ghislane make for the exit

Christopher I really don't think we need two tins of spam somehow, Al.

Al Corned beef. I must find it.

Elinor, on the other side of the stage, and Al watch Christopher and Ghislane leave

She looks fabulous, doesn't she, Ghislane, really glowing, alive.

Elinor Naturally, it's the happiest time of her life.

Al and Elinor are alone. Elinor is not facing him

Al Elinor ... did you get my note?

Elinor (*turning*) Yes. (*After a pause, quietly*) It was one of the most shocking things I've ever read.

Al (*chastened*) Is that what you think?

Elinor (*suddenly looking straight at him*) How can you begin to conceive that he has done such a thing?

Al (*nervously*) I don't know how I can either … but I'm beginning to feel fairly sure he has——

Elinor Christopher! Who's already successful! What possible reason do you think he would have for doing something so idiotic? (*Very sharply*) Why would he do that, Albie?

Al I don't know. *I don't know*. (*He moves*) Fame, perhaps.

Elinor Rubbish, don't be so banal, *that* is truly banal.

Al Well, people do strange things for celebrity now. You read about young artists killing themselves because they're not famous by the time they're thirty! Maybe Christopher wanted it so *badly*.

Elinor Oh, come on, for goodness sake—you may find it possible to imagine that about Christopher, but I can't.

Al Competition, then—he heard somebody else was getting close.

Elinor Nonsense, we both know at the moment there is no-one else anywhere near the Sun Battery.

Al We can't be sure about that, clearly! Or money—there's so much at stake, the *money*——

Elinor Christopher's never been interested in money.

Al With respect——

Elinor (*icily*) Yes?

Al (*facing up to her; very nervously*) You don't go out much, you may not be aware of the pressures. The commercial pressures.

Elinor I don't move around a lot, Albie, as you keep pointing out—but that doesn't mean I'm out of touch! (*Very sharply*) And explain to me how Christopher planned to make money out of this, if it's a fake? (*She stares at him*) That is just such sloppy thinking.

Al I admit these explanations are too easy. But I'm working on it.

Elinor I bet you are.

Al (*excited, loudly*) Well, something's happened! I *asked* him directly. I had to ask him just now. *And I didn't believe him*. (*He moves*) And that makes things very difficult…

Elinor (*rolling a cigarette*) Albie, calm down … please.

Pause. A prolonged burst of computer games sounds

Al So what do I do, Elinor?

Elinor Do? You do nothing.

Slight pause

Al (*surprised*) Nothing? But I think Barbara is going to talk to me about what
has occurred. If I get evidence…
Elinor You still do nothing.

The zigzagging sound of the computers. Then silence. Al is truly startled

Al Even if I get evidence.
Elinor I don't think that's remotely likely. And any evidence will be
challengeable. (*She pauses*) But even then, yes.
Al (*amazed*) What?
Elinor Yes. (*She calmly rolls a cigarette*) If, and I don't believe there is an
if, but if anything inexplicable has occurred, it has happened with us
knowing Christopher is very very close … the notes he's let us see
indicated there's definitely new work there.

Al stares at her

By the time he feels it right to publish it will be very clear how he's done
it. And the people round the world who are waiting right now to reproduce
the experiment, will be able to do so and applaud his achievement.

Silence

Al (*stunned, quietly*) Elinor … are you saying if he hasn't done it, at least he's
near, *so it doesn't matter if he's forged the results…*?
Elinor *You* are saying he hasn't done it—I am saying I know he is near.
Al I can't believe you mean that, Elinor.
Elinor I do mean it.
Al (*erupting*) For Chrissake, if we start thinking like that, everything goes,
doesn't it? Everything we believe in! (*He moves rapidly*) One can
announce I've discovered a cure for all forms of cancer, or AIDS, or I've
saved the world from a new killer bacteria … I have! I truly have! Well,
almost. In fact, what I should have said is I *nearly* have—except I've
cheated. I've forged a few results along the way—*in fact it's all a fake*.
Elinor (*steely*) I'm not saying that, Albie—and you know I'm not.
Al (*in disbelief*) No?
Elinor I'm saying there are things here you don't understand.
Al That's true!
Elinor And by giving them time, they'll clarify themselves.
Al You are saying ignore it, *even* if I have evidence. I *can't believe* you are
arguing that, Elinor, you've spent your whole life setting standards, being
an example to others——
Elinor I've spent my whole life resisting obvious explanations, because they

are invariably wrong. (*She looks up*) I've had to learn the importance of waiting——

Al (*suddenly*) It's a con, don't you realize? An idea that sounds so pure, sunlight and water, is a fucking con. He's used baking powder, for Chrissake! It's as crude as that. As sleazy as that.

Elinor (*implacably*) I don't believe it. That is totally impossible. Quite impossible. (*She pauses*) That certainly hasn't happened.

Silence. She looks at him. We hear the sound of the computer games outside

Albie, I have known you nearly half your life. I have taught you.

Al (*watching; quietly*) Tried to teach me.

Elinor Tried to teach you, yes. (*She smokes*) I probably know you as well as anyone—and I'm telling you this is not the time to intervene. There will be a professional and scientific explanation, of that I'm certain.

Al Will there?

Elinor I am convinced there will be. But if you blunder in now, with your flair for popularising things——

Al Yes. I know I'm a hack, but that's not the point——

Elinor —you will generate all kinds of media coverage, naturally. And that will have a devastating effect on Christopher's reputation...

Al And if it comes out I had prior knowledge of the deception——

Elinor There has been no deception, Albie.

Al If it comes out I had proof and did nothing——

Elinor Yes?

Al Then the whole department is finished. That doesn't matter?

Elinor I don't think you have a choice, Albie.

Silence

(*Softly*) Do you understand the situation better now?

Al Yes. You're forbidding me from doing anything.

Elinor Don't be silly, Albie—how can I forbid you? That's childish.

Silence

Come here...

Al moves up to her. She touches his hair

(*Much more gently, softly*) You look awful, unwashed, unkempt. (*She looks at his shirt*) This is filthy.

Al Yes, I've been sleeping in my clothes. There's probably a special mould growing here—a new strain of penicillin.

Elinor suddenly becomes intense, the whole strength of her personality

Elinor I'm telling you—from all my experience from everything I've learnt—I'm telling you ... you must not act. *You must not do it.*

Pause. The computer sounds, lazy rhythms, music drifting

(*Gently*) You've got many qualities, Albie, you've got to concentrate on what you do best, what comes naturally—your gift for organization, for planning.
Al (*quietly*) Yes.
Elinor Are you going to listen?

Pause

Al Yes.
Elinor Good. That's good. (*She moves*) Come on, then, chip chop. We've a picnic to attend. (*She smiles*) Imagine them all lying in the long grass, guzzling. If we leave it any later, they'll have eaten all the food. (*She moves*) We can go in my car.
Al No. I just need a moment to see to something. I'll drive myself. I know where it is.
Elinor OK, right. Super. (*She moves to exit*) See you under the trees.

Elinor exits

Al is alone. He moves slowly

Al (*quietly*) Jesus...

Joanna enters, carrying her bag

Joanna I knew you'd still be here.

Al only looks up

You're not going to the picnic, are you?
Al (*preoccupied*) What? No, I can't.
Joanna And we're not going away together?
Al (*concentrating deeply*) What?
Joanna (*laughing*) Well, that couldn't be clearer. (*Lightly*) I was stupid to expect anything else, wasn't I?

Al grunts deep in thought

I thought so. I'll have to settle for this. (*She touches him gently*) Whatever this is. (*She smiles*) I don't think this is very much. (*She moves*) Sometimes I think you're only interested in me because we met on the day you became Professor—I'm really just a memento, and will end up in a plastic bag. (*She stares at him*) Come on, Al, what's the matter?

Al looks up

Since you're obviously not thinking about me at all.

Al (*quietly*) No. (*He looks at Joanna, very preoccupied*) The old bastard was right. Elinor was no help.

Joanna You told her about Christopher?

Al Yes ... the most scrupulous person I've ever known, the great Elinor— and she told me to do nothing.

Joanna And what did you say?

Al I just reverted ... I couldn't prevent it. I became the pupil again.

Pause

Joanna She probably needs a little time to take it all in.

Al No, *no*. That is not what is happening.

Joanna (*burrowing in her bag*) By the way, Barbara gave me this notebook—where is it?—a little thing with a rose on it... Here, she asked me to give it to you. (*She hands him the book*) She said you'd understand.

Al Yes, I was expecting it.

Joanna Aren't you going to look at it?

Al I know what it'll show. (*He flicks the pages, but he's not really looking at it*) It's evidence. She will have written what she saw. (*He flicks the pages again, this time looking for longer*) Shit! Yes! (*He lets out a yell of rage*) I can't ignore this!

Joanna It's difficult, of course, for you, Al. (*She watches him*) But you did a piece of detective work—and you came up with a result.

Al I wasn't expecting to! I really didn't *want* to be right! (*He pauses*) I still don't know why it's happened. (*He paces*) It's like I've put the pieces of the jigsaw together, and I'm staring at it now, and I don't know what it shows. Except Christopher's finished. *However* it's presented to the world, whatever euphemism is used, he's finished. But I don't know why it's happened. (*He moves round the stage*) What do I keep from here? From this bloody morning? (*He moves, intense*) The day of the celebratory picnic. What lousy little thing should I keep? So I remember *exactly* what it was like. (*He stares across at Joanna*) I wish somebody would rumble me. Tap me on the shoulder and say OK, that's it. We know you're pint-sized, you're here by accident. *We'll* take care of it from now on. You've

done enough. (*He moves again. Then stops*) Rumble me … come on, for
Chrissake… Rumble me!

The Lights fade

ACT II

SCENE 1

Al is facing us, with a larger plastic container at his feet

Al A good place to restart, I think, is with this. (*He gives the bag a nudge*) Somewhere in the intervening four years I'd graduated to bigger bags… (*He turns the bag round slowly*) We have gone right past that colour supplement—with us on the cover—and reached this. (*He pulls in his stomach*) Despite my best efforts, I'd grown a little fatter too—just a touch. (*He prizes open the bag*) So what do we have…? (*He looks inside in silence*) Strange smells. (*He pauses*) We find a load of audio tapes, of my own voice. Well, why not? A fistful of press cuttings and… (*He produces it with a flourish*) And a fork—pinched from the Garrick Club! (*He stares at the fork for a moment*) I was very busy … hectic days … and in the middle of it all, I kept on getting invited by that old villain Brownhill for lunch at his club.

Al exits

The Professor and Joanna are sitting side by side in deep armchairs. Joanna is dressed fashionably but impersonally. She seems older, more sophisticated. She is very ill at ease, though, sitting, waiting with the Professor

Professor You won't recognize him.

Joanna Won't I? I haven't been away that long!

Professor As soon as he comes in, you will see a considerable difference. He struts.

Joanna Struts! Really? I can't imagine Al strutting.

Professor And God, does he work. Not real work, of course, mostly admin, but he beavers away——

Joanna Well, he's always beavered, worked harder than he made out.

Professor His snout in here, his snout in there. I don't resent him. We need his sort. Everybody finds Albert useful—I was right. (*He looks around, smiles*) You know he gives these little talks on the radio now.

Joanna (*amused*) He doesn't? What about?

Professor Oh yes, before the news in the morning. Only five minutes, mind you. (*With a slight laugh*) That's quite long enough for Albert's thoughts! What used to be called the God slot. (*With an admiring smile*) Load of balls, of course.

Al enters

(*Totally unfazed*) There you are. I was just saying, one can't open a newspaper or switch on the radio, without hearing your voice.

Al Rubbish, William. You exaggerate. (*He stares at Joanna*) Hallo, Joanna.

Joanna Hi, Al.

Al (*warmly*) Hi! (*He leans over and kisses her*)

Professor Still to conquer TV, of course. But that will come next no doubt.

Joanna (*as Al kisses her, whispering*) I didn't realize we weren't going to be alone.

Al (*whispering*) I'll explain later. (*Louder*) You look wonderful!

Joanna I feel wonderful-ish.

Professor You won't when it starts filling up here. The members rolling in, muttering to themselves.

Joanna Well, you certainly look successful, Al.

Al Do I? (*Intimately*) You look so different, Joanna.

Professor He's written a book too, *Beware of the Experts*, crude but effective, pandering to the young. Give us veterans a good hiding. (*He smiles*) It's selling really well, of course.

Joanna (*to Al*) You never sent me a copy.

Al (*intimately, urgently*) I hope you've kept all afternoon for me, say you have. *Please*, it's important. (*He is close to her, touches her arm*)

Joanna (*with a warm laugh*) That depends!

Professor But it's not just media claptrap. He's on a number of committees too.

Al Anybody can be on a committee, especially if you offer to do the minutes——

Joanna Anything of importance?

Professor Oh, yes.

Al (*embarrassed, laughing*) Jesus! Stop! He's like my agent, isn't he?

Joanna You have an agent too?

Professor Albert's on quite a vital committee, grading science departments in universities round the country——

Al (*grinning broadly*) He likes to think "you see what I've unleashed on the world".

Professor Half horrified, of course! (*He chuckles*) More than half.

Al (*returning to Joanna, softly*) You're marvellously brown, how did you get to look like this in New York in the winter? Is this how you look all the time?

Joanna Oh no, this is just for you, Albert, of course! (*Suddenly*) Have you done fraud, by any chance, in one of your five minute talks?

Pause

Al Scientific fraud? No.

Joanna No?

Professor Oh, you mean Christopher—there've been endless articles by all sorts of riff-raff, most of them with awful titles, like "The Baking Powder Fraud", colour supplement stuff.

Al But not by me, and not about why it happened, which is the important question, nobody's bothered yet——

Professor (*cutting him off*) No, Al's not cashed in directly, hasn't written a book about Christopher. But once he found himself in the spotlight, he made damn sure he stayed there, didn't you, Albert?

Al (*startled by this*) Thank you!

Joanna Have you *seen* Christopher?

Al No. (*After a slight pause*) I hear he's managing.

Joanna He is? And how is Elinor?

Al (*smiling*) Oh, she's even more like Elinor than usual—still eating the barley sugars.

Professor I can tell you what happened with Christopher...

Al stops, surprised

Joanna You can?

Professor It's quite simple, he was always a nonentity.

Al No, that's not the case!

Professor Oh, yes, a nonentity. He wanted to lie his way to the top, because deep down he knew he wasn't good enough.

Al (*becoming angry*) Christopher was not a nonentity!

Professor (*glibly*) He had a humble background—he was desperate to succeed.

Al (*his anger bursting out*) That is not true. You want to play this game, solve the mystery, then you have to get your bloody facts right! Christopher's the son of a country doctor, as it happens, a very happy childhood. (*Loudly*) The solution doesn't lie there, I assure you!

A startled pause

Professor Maybe not, Albert. You're the authority on people, after all. But the result's the same, isn't it? (*He gets up*) As I get older I get much less forgiving, I'm afraid. (*To Joanna*) I've said my piece, now I must relieve

myself. You will excuse me, my dear. Soon you will have the benefit of
our gruesome cuisine, overcooked beyond belief. (*He makes to exit*) I hope
you're not too hungry.

Professor exits

Joanna Thank God he's gone for a moment. I didn't realize he was quite *that*
loathsome.

Al That's him on a good day!

Joanna He hates everything, doesn't he? (*She laughs*) He even hates the
food.

Al For some reason he doesn't hate *me*—which is worrying.

Pause. He stares at her

(*Very warmly*) So here we are, Joanna. Both pretty *OK*.

Joanna (*smiling*) Yes, that's right.

Al (*close, intimate*) How's the job?

Joanna (*laughing*) I can't believe it! A question about *my* work. It's good—
I'm working as a publicist now.

Al A publicist!

Joanna Don't say it like that.

Al The Hype Industry.

Joanna Yes, but it's not just that. We concentrate on the arts. Publishing.
(*She smiles*) Maybe we'll be handling your books.

Al I'm sure. (*He looks at her for a moment*) That thesis you wrote—"The
Impact of the Invention of Detergent"—that was very memorable, Joanna.

Joanna Memorable! You've never said that before.

Al Oh, yes. (*He grins*) I often think about it. How we met. You were so
confident—you showed great originality in being interested in that.

Joanna You want something, Al, what is it?

Al (*softly*) I've missed you terribly.

Joanna Of course you have, once every eighteen months.

Al No, no.

Joanna So much, I didn't even qualify for a meal on my own. (*Very direct*)
So what is it?

Al lowers his voice

Al I didn't want to say this in front of the Professor, but…

Joanna Say what?

Al (*glancing around*) I have to be quick, his pee breaks are disappointingly
short. (*His tone is hushed, urgent*) I may be going to see Christopher very
soon. First time since … next week, at the university.

Joanna Great. I'm sure you should.
Al And I want *you* to come with me.
Joanna (*startled*) Why? This is surely something you've got to do on your own.
Al No. I want you to be there. It's important, I have an agenda.
Joanna An agenda? What does that mean?
Al *I am going to put the pieces back together*, before my luck runs out. It's bound to be difficult. Mission impossible maybe. But *I can do it*. Christopher is very practical—I think he sees me as somebody who in fact contained the storm, who didn't call in professionals to break the fraud, but handled it myself.

Pause. He stares at her

And I need *your* advice really badly.
Joanna Don't overdo it, Al, it doesn't suit you.
Al OK. (*After a slight pause, he smiles*) I'm too much of a coward to do it on my own. Is that better?
Joanna Yes. (*She smiles warmly*) That's a little better.

Black-out

SCENE 2

The green faded walls of the department

There are two vending machines now, the old Sixties one, and a much newer model, its neon display shining out. There are cafeteria tables, chairs upturned on one of them

Charlie is standing behind the service area

Elinor is eating out of a pudding bowl

Elinor A little more custard, Charlie.
Charlie That's your third one, Dr Brickman.
Elinor (*lightly*) Don't argue, just go ahead and do it. And make it a big dollop, this time...

Charlie pours the custard

...No—*bigger*. (*She smiles*) Super. Thank you.

Joanna enters

Joanna (*quietly, tentatively*) Hi, Elinor...

Elinor turns

Elinor (*startled*) Oh, goodness... (*She pauses for a moment*) Hallo, stranger. What brings you here?

Joanna I'm not sure. (*With a nervous laugh*) I mean, Al is here, he wanted me to come. I'm sorry—of course I'm *glad* to be here.

Elinor (*eating her custard*) There's no need to apologise, we're delighted to see you, aren't we, Charlie?

Charlie Delighted.

Joanna I'm not disturbing you?

Elinor No, no, this is my custard break. Every evening at the same time, lots and lots of it.

Charlie She's becoming addicted.

Elinor Absolutely. (*Calmly, easily*) The most attractive man I've ever met— so far—happened over a shared bowl of custard ... it's always been a very sexy substance for me.

Joanna (*with a startled laugh*) Elinor, I'm surprised.

Elinor Yes. (*She eats*) In fact I've started a campaign—Charlie and I are planning to reintroduce all the desserts and sweets of our childhood into this cafeteria, aren't we ... gobstoppers and tons and tons of sherbet. (*She smiles*) Gleefully putting the clock back. (*She looks up from the bowl*) So where is Albie?

Joanna He's just coming. Any moment. He's been rushing around visiting people.

Elinor We haven't seen him for a while, he's been very occupied I believe with his articles, his books, his talks. (*Very deadpan*) I heard one actually, a radio talk, it was about a weighty and important topic—why cats' urine, or should I say cats' piss, smells so much.

Charlie laughs

No, it was.

Charlie As bad as that! He has fought for the department, though, hasn't he, protected it.

Elinor Yes. Well, that is what he's there for.

Charlie Managed to limit the damage after the Occurrence.

Elinor (*with a slight laugh*) Charlie always refers to it as the "Occurrence".

Charlie Yes. And the Occurrence is over now—the effects. I'm sure they are.

Joanna Christopher's meant to be coming, isn't he?
Elinor Well, if Albie is here, I doubt it. But one never knows. Christopher travels a lot, his arrangements change.
Joanna (*watching her closely*) And how are things here?
Elinor Good. Very good. (*She looks up*) You know, Charlie and I—we've been here the longest of anyone. Charlie six months less than me.
Charlie Fifty-seven. I was here in May fifty-seven.
Elinor (*laughing*) And you looked ancient even then!
Charlie Yes, well, it means I haven't changed, doesn't it! Of course it was a sit-down service then, rather grand.
Elinor (*putting the custard bowl down*) That was delicious.
Joanna Have you finished your work?

Elinor stops

Elinor I haven't finished, no.
Joanna Are you near?
Elinor (*lightly*) You sound like Albie.
Joanna I didn't mean to pry.
Elinor No, it's fine—sometimes it seems jolly near, and other moments I'm not so sure. But in a few months, probably, something will appear. I still stalk the passages at night, don't I, Charlie?
Charlie Yes, I see her pass by, just as I leave for the night.

Al's voice is heard in the passage, calling out, greeting someone

Elinor Oh, goodness, so there he is already. (*She pushes the chair into the table and moves in the opposite direction*)
Joanna What are you doing? Don't go. He's coming to see you.
Elinor I know. I'm not avoiding him, I promise. (*She smiles*) But my custard break is over. And Albie is much better faced in the morning, that's always been the case.

Elinor exits

Al enters, a second after Elinor has exited. He carries a large black rubbish bag, stuffed with papers

He looks around, surprised

Al I thought for a moment…
Joanna Elinor was here. She was. She had to go. She's looking forward to seeing you in the morning.

Al grunts, puts the rubbish bag down on the table, papers pouring out of it

What's that grunt mean?
Al One moment, I just need to, these are some of my old papers, just checking… Just refreshing. (*He is lost in thought*)
Joanna What is this? What's so important suddenly?
Al (*hardly audibly, grunting*) Just a moment.
Joanna (*lightly*) This is some compliment! (*To Charlie*) He begs me to come with him and then he does this! Hallo? (*She moves close, touching him*) What's going on, Al?
Al (*hardly audibly, grunting*) One more minute.
Joanna (*laughing*) Thanks! Of course, that explains everything. (*She moves*) To think I let the last precious moments of my "youth" dribble away among the smells of this department. (*To Charlie*) No disrespect intended! (*She touches Al's head*) But I was rewarded by witnessing something special. (*She pauses slightly*) Not today!

Al grunts

Tonight of all nights—he starts playing the mad professor! Oh, Al.
Al (*sharply*) Just one moment, please, I just have to… (*His voice tails away*)
Joanna (*lightly*) Fuck it. (*To Charlie*) If he ever notices I've gone—I'll be in the bar.

Joanna exits

Al doesn't see. Silence. Charlie is having his cigarette break, standing by the food

Al (*with papers*) Forgotten how to do this, it's been so long. I have to stick my tongue out to concentrate, like a school kid. (*He suddenly looks up*) Joanna?
Charlie She went.
Al She went? (*He pauses slightly*) That helps for a moment. (*His tone changes, becomes more expansive*) Do you believe in Eureka moments, Charlie?
Charlie You mean moments of sudden discovery, sir?
Al Yes, like in a cartoon—the light bulb coming out of a head, bang! (*He smiles, looking at Charlie*) A moment like that?
Charlie I'm not sure I've ever seen one, sir. (*With a laconic grin*) Despite all the eminent talent that's filed right past me in this cafeteria.
Al Nor have I. Till now. (*He gets up*) This is not strictly speaking a Eureka moment.

Charlie What? (*He grins*) There is one happening in here—now? (*Startled*) With you, sir?
Al Amazing as it may seem, yes. It's not a pure Eureka moment—because I've had this idea for several weeks, ever since I found these old notes of mine—from my younger self, surprisingly bright in fact. They got me thinking…

Pause. He moves round the formica table

But this is the nearest I'll ever get to a Eureka moment. (*He flicks the papers*) Let me see if it works again.
Charlie Shall I get anybody else to witness this?
Al No, no. This is just for you, Charlie. I'm not ready for a bigger audience. This *is me* doing it, after all! (*He stands by the table*) It doesn't sound very prepossessing—it is to do with *garbage*. Rubbish, waste… (*He looks at Charlie*) No obvious jokes, please.
Charlie Did I say anything, sir?
Al *Garbage*—extracting workable fuel, a form of petrol, from household waste. That you can run vehicles on. It is not quite as big an idea as the Sun Battery, but it could be very important. (*He smiles*) Maybe. (*He moves to the table*) Give me that, please, Charlie.

Charlie passes him the ladle, and Al scoops some baked beans straight out onto the table, beginning to form a diagram with them, smudging them across the table top

If this is the raw material, one would have to grind it … grind… (*He grinds the beans for a moment*) Then… (*He takes some mushy peas, and expands the diagram*) Then mix with water containing the catalyst, with vital rhodium catalyst … and then … give me those burgers, Charlie. (*He ladles some very overcooked burgers onto the table, and into the diagram*) You add hydrogen gas and then the co-catalyst phosphene. (*He ladles some sweetcorn on*) Do you see the shape? The shape, Charlie? (*He moves with the ladle*) Allow it to cool, release the pressure. (*He sprinkles some chips on top*) And the fuel will be floating on the top. Like so… (*He sprinkles more chips*) Like so. Give me some more … more burgers, Charlie … they're cooked to a crisp, aren't they! More mushy peas … if we could. (*He stares at the table-top*) If only we could… (*He sprinkles some more chips*) It is, of course, round the mushy peas that it is still unclear, it is incomplete. If I put in a lot of work round the mushy peas, Charlie, it will become clearer, it will be achieved.
Charlie It sounds fantastic.
Al (*grinning boyishly*) It *could* be fantastic.

Elinor's music is heard in the distance

Charlie An apple-falling-off-a-tree moment?
Al No, not quite, Charlie. (*He smiles*) Undoubtedly the messiest Eureka
moment there's ever been … I think we can claim the prize!
Charlie We could still celebrate, couldn't we? You deserve a drink. Shall
we go to the bar, sir?
Al That's an excellent idea, Charlie. But I need to do this now—if I'm going
to get it ready for the others. (*He moves to the end of the table with the
papers*) Have to find a space where there are no beans. (*He sits studiously
at the end of the table*)

Elinor's music is heard in the background

It's funny, when the place is coming to an end—this happens.
Charlie (*sharply*) Coming to an end?
Al I shouldn't have said that. You didn't hear me. The committee has made
some decisions but nothing is official. *You* won't be affected, Charlie. But
I may no longer have to concern myself with this place. (*He smiles*) The
weight is lifted. (*He works with the papers*) I plan to involve the others with
this idea, of course.
Charlie Dr Christopher and Dr Elinor?
Al Yes. Form a unit, with them, somewhere else. It'll be a powerful set-up.
(*He bends over the papers*) This is real work, Charlie, for a change! Do you
hear Elinor's music? (*He writes*) Do you think Christopher will come?
Charlie I expect so. He'll want to see you, after all this time.
Al I'm not sure he'll want to exactly! But he'll be curious. (*He smiles*)

Charlie, cleaning up, begins to wipe the table, the baked beans diagram

Don't, Charlie, leave it! I need that! Don't wipe anything, please! Put those
back at once. (*He grins*) I'm using it.

Charlie flicks the beans off the cloth, back on the table

Charlie (*amused*) I beg your pardon, sir, forgive me.
Al (*more seriously*) If it could work, Charlie, Jesus! (*He begins to write*) I'm
trying to get it into a presentable form for tomorrow, so they can give their
comments. Elinor's a very tough judge, of course.

Pause

Being able to hear her music, it's like you can sense her thought process.

I'll work all night if necessary. I am here, and she is working just down the passage. It's as if we're working in unison for the first time.

Black-out

SCENE 3

Elinor's laboratory. Early evening of the following day

A portion of the scientific apparatus she uses comes on. It looks almost sculptural, as it bends along one side of the stage

The sun is reddening, then going down during the scene, and various lamps are switched on, dotted around the lab

From outside come the sounds of students' parties, from other buildings in the university. At the beginning of the scene, the sound is quite faint, a gentle noise of distant music

Ghislane is standing with Christopher. There is a contrast in their manner, even the colour of their clothes. Ghislane in dark colours, nervous, fidgety, her hair has begun to turn grey. Christopher is in a summer suit, and a seemingly expansive, confident mood

Christopher It's amazing.
Ghislane What is?
Christopher That old bicycle with the broken front wheel is still there— after all this time. (*He turns*) I saw Bogle just now, he's lost almost all his hair.
Ghislane I don't think I've ever been in here before, Elinor never encouraged visitors.

We hear the sound of Al's voice in the passage

(*Nervously*) She'll be here, won't she? I thought Elinor said she definitely was going to be here, for the moment when we meet Al.
Christopher (*very calmly*) She'll be here. I saw her earlier today... (*He laughs*) We had an orange juice together—she doesn't change.

Al and Joanna enter. Al is wearing stylish clothes, a rather fashionable tie

Silence for a split second

Al.
Al Christopher.
Christopher (*in a bantering tone*) Nice tie!
Al (*grinning*) Well, it's a reunion tie. (*He smiles*) For *this* reunion. I spent a ridiculously long time choosing it.
Ghislane Hallo, Joanna.
Joanna Hi.
Christopher (*casually*) Yes, hallo. (*Only focusing on Al*) Have you had your hair tinted, Al? I think you have.
Al No, I have not!
Christopher It looks lighter, a little tint definitely.
Al (*laughing*) I have not had it tinted!
Joanna Unless somebody did it in your sleep.
Al Must be the sun.

Christopher watches him

Christopher Yes, I hear it's been a good spring in England. For once.
Al Yes. So far. April's been very good, May has started well. (*Suddenly*) We're not going to talk about the weather, are we? (*He laughs*) Fucking hell—we meet again and talk about the *weather*.
Christopher (*lightly*) But you're very good at talking about the weather—aren't you, Al?
Al What do you mean?
Ghislane The only one of your radio talks we've heard…
Christopher Was about the weather.
Ghislane I think its theme was—contrary to popular belief we don't talk about the weather *enough*. (*She smiles*) It was quite impressive, very confident.
Al (*smiling*) Confident bullshit, yes.

Pause

Christopher And in Japan, I was browsing in a bookshop, when suddenly your perky face was staring back at me, it was your book *Beware of the Experts*—in Japanese.
Al In Japan! Really? (*With a self-mocking laugh*) It was probably remaindered, wasn't it?
Christopher (*easily*) Must be a very different sort of lecture tour, promoting pop-science books.
Ghislane Plenty of good hotels.
Al Yes…
Joanna And girls no doubt. Plenty of them!

Al No, no, I'm planning to settle down. My daughter who is a real young lady now—doesn't approve.

Christopher (*lightly, ignoring this*) Bad science—great sex. Al's little buttocks going up and down in hotel rooms all over the world.

Al (*laughing*) Maybe we should get back to talking about the weather, quick!

Silence. Al moves

Christopher... Did you get a chance? (*He stops*) Did you find an envelope pushed under your door this morning?

Christopher An envelope. (*Lightly*) I might have done.

Pause

Al So have you had time to look at it?

Christopher flicks his fingers, Ghislane produces a tape recorder

What's that for?

Christopher Just for the record.

Al What record?

Ghislane So everything is absolutely clear.

Christopher No possibilities whatsoever of any distortions.

Al What?

Ghislane It is *my* advice. My legal advice.

Al (*in disbelief*) We can't talk with this here—it's like a police interview.

Christopher (*calmly*) Well, that's rather appropriate, isn't it, Al—I saw you described somewhere as a science policeman.

Al Christopher. (*He paces*) We don't need it, we really don't ... this is *you and me*.

Christopher (*calmly*) We just don't want you misrepresenting this conversation in any way—for popular consumption. (*He smiles*) It's no big deal, you'll soon forget it's here.

Al Jesus! OK, it stays. For the moment. (*He moves, with a slight laugh*)

Silence

So what do you think? Of the idea? What do you *really think*?

Slight pause

Christopher Fuel out of household garbage? Using those two catalysts ... the rhodium and... (*He stops*) You want my honest opinion?

Al (*very quietly*) Yes.

Slight pause

Christopher (*with a slow smile*) I think it has possibilities.
Al (*startled*) Really? You do!
Christopher Yes … it's a sketch at the moment, of course.
Al Yes, yes! (*He laughs*) I will type it up properly, re-present it.
Christopher But it *is* a genuinely good idea.

Silence

Joanna That's great, isn't it, Al? (*With an affectionate laugh*) An idea of your own!
Al (*quietly*) Yes—it's tremendous. (*He pauses. In an urgent tone*) I tell you what I want to do, I want to form a *unit* to help develop the idea—and *others*.

Christopher smiles

Please listen to this. (*He moves*) Do *you* want to be involved? (*He grins, indicating the tape recorder*) With or without a constant record.
Christopher (*quietly*) Involved in your unit?
Al You could rework the Sun Battery, explore further, keeping it rather low profile at first, of course … but *after a time…*

Christopher smiles a distant smile

I want it to be a powerhouse, a real Powerhouse of Ideas, Christopher.

Elinor enters

Elinor Oh, good, everybody's here already. (*She smiles*) I've missed all the awkward bits.
Al That's right!
Christopher You're in time for something else, though.
Al Hi, Elinor.
Elinor Albie. (*She pauses slightly*) It's very good to see you.
Al Yes—and it's a lovely idea to have this meeting in *your* lab, because I've hardly ever been allowed in it before.
Elinor So you keep reminding me, Albie. (*She pauses and glances around*) Well, we all look much the same, don't we? That's rather refreshing—no shocks. (*She smiles*) Or maybe it's a little disappointing, perhaps we should have all changed dramatically! (*She moves*) Anybody want some coffee?
Al Yes, I'll make it.

Elinor No, no, it has to be found first. It's kept in a disgusting old tin in the passage… (*She smiles*) To deter anybody from stealing it. It needs me to find it. (*She moves, glancing at Al and Christopher*) A little coffee, and then we can start to function properly.

Elinor exits

Silence

Christopher (*smiling calmly*) Albert—it may seem a charming thought to try to put the pieces together, but the last thing, the very last thing I want is for you to have any control over my actions—as a moment's thought might have told you.

Al I wouldn't have control…

Christopher And it's not necessary either. Nothing has *changed* for me.

Al Nothing has changed?! Come on, Christopher.

Christopher Not when one looks at the *facts*.

Al You don't have to pretend here, please.

Christopher Pretend! What kind of word is that? There is no pretence.

Ghislane What Christopher means is—things are almost repaired, after a long process of——

Christopher (*cutting her off*) I know what I mean. (*His tone is effortlessly calm*) No, I have no need for any of this, Al, but I'll be very interested if you repeat your offer to Elinor… (*He look straight at him*) Since one of the main reasons you are here, is to tell her you're shutting down her lab— terminating her.

Joanna What? What is this, Al?

Al It's not as simple as that. Elinor and I have to have a talk——

Christopher Clearly.

Ghislane That's one way of putting it.

Al —and I have to tell her about the unit, of course.

Joanna So that's why you were so eager for me to be here with you— because you knew there was going to be unpleasantness.

Al No! I wanted us all to meet again for several reasons, but primarily to see if we could *resume*.

Joanna Jesus, Al, I can't believe this! I thought I'd come to watch things being mended, at a reunion.

Christopher suddenly looks at her

Christopher (*very calmly*) I'm sorry, but you didn't, you came out of voyeurism, didn't you? To see what I looked like now.

Joanna (*startled*) What?

Christopher To see how I appeared. (*He smiles*) It's perfectly understandable.

Joanna Thanks! (*With a nervous laugh*) I think I can do without this! (*She moves*) OK...?

Christopher There is absolutely no need to be upset. I'm not in the least angry you came. I would have done the same.

Joanna No. I shouldn't be here. I don't belong here now. (*She moves off*) Al, please think about what you're doing.

Al It'll be *all right. Don't worry...*

Elinor enters with a battered old tin

Elinor Coffee, at last. And we can pig ourselves on ginger biscuits.

Al Great.

Joanna Elinor, I just need to do something, I'll be back soon ... OK.

Elinor Don't be long.

Joanna exits

Slight pause

Christopher It turns out Al has a couple of things to put to you, Elinor.

Elinor Oh, good. I usually react with interest to what Albie has to say.

Christopher This is of particular interest. And while he's doing that, I think I have some calls to make.

Al You're not going too?

Ghislane (*hastily*) Yes, we have a flight to Germany tomorrow. He's been working very hard.

Christopher Of course. I'm truly busy. There have been times recently when I've just put the phone down, and it has rung immediately, without even a second's delay. I have invitations bulging through the letter-box every morning. (*He smiles*) Funnily enough, I even get invited to places I was never invited to before.

Al Christopher...

Christopher Maybe out of notoriety, who knows. My life has never been quite so full... (*He grins*) Which is odd, isn't it! That's what you did, Al— and I'm not even angry.

Al I think I'd feel happier if you were screaming at me.

Christopher There is no need for that. You thought you had a job to do, it could have done harm, but it *did* not.

Al (*impatiently, urgently*) Christopher, for God's sake! This is me here...

Christopher No, the truth is, listen to the truth, Al, because it's interesting— a temporary adjustment to my career was required, that's all. I bear no ill will, even to that girl, I can't remember her name now, who thought she had evidence. If time and money had allowed, maybe I should have sued, and cleared up everything in the courts. But the moment's passed.

Ghislane (*trying to stop him*) We better check our departure times now. (*She moves*)

Al Christopher! *I want to know why!*

Christopher (*calmly turning*) I know you want an admission, a confession even. But there is nothing to admit, Al. I just couldn't repeat the experiment, that's all. (*He moves*) It's very simple really. (*He smiles*) Don't think about it any further. I know it's galling—*but there is nothing more to discover.*

Christopher exits with Ghislane

Pause

Elinor Well, they certainly don't want to drink my coffee. (*She smiles and looks at the disgusting tin*) Maybe it's the container.

Al He was amazing—he did it so effortlessly. (*He pauses*) He was so like Christopher! Never letting the mask slip.

Elinor He was bound to be like that. Naturally, seeing you again.

Al Yes, of course.

Elinor It may change in time between you and him. You never know.

Al It will.

Elinor (*watching him*) So the sole reason for this visit, Albie, is for you to see Christopher?

Al Yes—and you, of course.

Elinor stares across at him for a second. Her manner is soft and informal, seemingly on her best behaviour for Albie

Elinor Oh, yes, to see *me*. (*She puts the tin down*) I've got a better idea. (*She moves to the cupboard*) I have a bottle of whisky somewhere.

Al A drink—in here! In the lab?

Elinor Oh, yes.

Al That's very unlike you.

Elinor Oh, no, it's not. (*She smiles*) There's a lot you don't know. (*She pours the whisky into china cups*) And it goes with the music—the pre-exam parties. The kids, hear them, last chance to indulge. That's the American Film Club's party.

Al You can tell the different parties—just by listening!

Elinor Yes. I've been working in this room so long, some of the music I used to hear out there has come back into fashion. I suddenly find myself transported back to the Sixties.

Al You should have taped the sound of all those parties through the years, be an incredible record!

Pause. He watches her, clears his throat

Did you have a chance to see the paper I pushed under the door early this morning?

Elinor I received it, yes.

Slight pause. Elinor drinks, already refilling the cup with more whisky

Al I gave you the original. (*He smiles*) That's why it was spattered with beans—I hope that didn't put you off.

Elinor Oh, it was baked beans, was it—I thought it was chicken curry. Anyway, I got it, complete with the beans. (*She moves the bottle of whisky, and points to the floor*) You see this—it's a very important stain, Albie. Crucial, the biggest here. Trifluoro-acetic acid. It's from 1967, when a very stormy love affair ended—rather suddenly! Yells and tears... (*She smiles*) The end of several relationships are marked all over here in fact, by different stains. (*She smiles*) The exact size depending on how intense they were! There's a whole patch just where you're standing! (*She laughs*) One could crawl on all fours around here in fact, and inspect my private life. (*She pauses and looks up at Al*) Some other time maybe?

Al (*casually, not interested*) I must take a look, Elinor, yes. (*Suddenly unable to wait any more*) So what do you think of the work, my paper? Tell me!

Pause

Elinor (*smiling*) Your "paper"—what I saw of it, through the baked beans?

Al Yes?

Elinor I thought it was great.

Pause as Al takes this in for a second, in disbelief

Al It is? Isn't it? (*He punches the air*) Yes! (*He moves, excited*) Never heard you call anything great before.

Elinor Maybe super, rather than great. Naturally it needs work—there are obvious gaps.

Al Of course, yes ... but as a start?

Elinor It's more than a start.

Al Yes? This is terrific ... Elinor, isn't it?

Pause. The sound of the parties

Elinor Was it, how shall I put this—all your own work, Albie?

Al (*lightly*) Amazing as it may seem, yes.

Elinor Nobody else contributed?

Al No.

Elinor (*sipping whisky*) Are you sure? Before the baked beans stage—there was nobody else?

Al Jesus, what is this? (*With a nervous laugh*) You think I stole it? You can't believe that, Elinor. (*He moves*) After all, it's not *me* who was found to be doing fraudulent experiments.

Pause

Elinor No, Albie. *That* you haven't done.

Al What does that mean?

Elinor No, no, I'm on my best behaviour tonight. (*She looks across at Al*) I'm trying to do myself some good here, aren't I?

Slight pause. She drinks. Al turns. Elinor lightens her tone

Hear that? It's another party starting ... that's the Poetry Society. The music's always very violent there.

Al (*calmly*) Please, Elinor—you must tell me exactly what you mean. You can't think I got it wrong about Christopher?

Elinor No. (*She moves the equipment*) I've just got to do this ... I am prepared to accept there were irregularities.

Al Irregularities.

Elinor That Christopher had a complete aberration. That I was wrong.

Al And I was right.

Elinor is by the equipment

Can I help? Can I be of assistance?

Elinor (*taking a sharp reading*) No. I've done it. (*She turns*) What I cannot accept, I have to tell you, is the way you have used what has happened— how everything that followed your discovery about Christopher has been passed off as a complete accident—but each time it's led to your advancement in some way.

Al I've only been doing what I've always done, Elinor, keeping my head above water. You know that's how it's happened.

Elinor Don't be absurd.

Al It's the truth.

Elinor (*calmly*) I don't just mean your silly talks on the radio, but how you've used the wave of anti-science feeling for your own purposes, feeding people's cynicism. And fear. According to you, not only are scientists solely responsible for buggering up the planet——

Al I don't believe that.

Elinor —but a great number of them aren't even any good. Exaggerating the

value of their work to get funding, etc. etc. And you've become a best-
selling author peddling that—it's brilliant! And a little nauseating.

Al (*watching her*) Go on.

Elinor You've always described yourself as a hack, Albie—but now you've
become slightly more dangerous. Somebody who reduces everything to
their own level—and does it very effectively.

Al My rise, Elinor—if it can be called that—*is* an accident, one haphazard
thing after another.

Elinor Of course.

Al I'm not upset.

Elinor (*more softly*) It takes a lot more to upset you, Albie, I know. (*She sips
the whisky*) Keep drinking…

Al And it will not influence me, in any way.

Elinor No?

Al I will just point out you haven't seen an awful lot of me recently.

Elinor (*very sharply, suddenly*) Oh, but I think I have, haven't I! Oh, yes,
very definitely.

Al What you mean, I haven't been here. What you talking about?

Elinor On the rare occasions I venture out, I see you all over the place, slices
of you, Al.

Al What?

Elinor Things that remind me of you—staring at me from the sides of buses,
from giant posters. One can't move anywhere without being urged to tailor
things to the marketplace, justify everything in commercial terms. (*She
moves*) I see you everywhere, Al, and I dread seeing you.

Al (*louder*) That is not true!

Elinor (*more lightly again*) Maybe you should reach the other thing you've
come to tell me, Albie.

More new music and party sounds

Al (*slowly, deliberately*) Elinor, when I started being in charge here, my
attitude wasn't entirely formed. What I've experienced at first hand since
then, has left me in no doubt that most work should be geared directly to
the marketplace… But it is a really crude analysis to think that's *all* I
believe in.

Elinor (*with her back to him, listening to the parties*) Is it?

Al It's caricature to say I'm just crassly commercial. *I* was the one who told
Christopher to slow down. (*Suddenly*) And you told me—unforgivably—
to ignore what I'd found! To forget it!

Elinor You misunderstood what I said, no doubt for your own reasons.

Al No. It still stuns me when I think about it, what you told me to do.

Elinor If that's what you want to believe.

Al That's what happened, for Chrissake—*those are the facts.*
Elinor If it helps you to think that, to justify your drive for efficiency.

Silence

Al Tell me, Elinor, have you had a new idea in twenty-five years?

Pause

Come on, tell me, I'm interested, a single fresh idea?
Elinor One or two, I believe, yes.
Al Name them. Come on, tell me. (*Very sharply*) Name just one.
Elinor This is stupid.
Al All this secrecy, all this proud isolation, which has got even worse
recently—and yet there isn't a shred of evidence that anything has been
produced here, is there! You can't expect nobody to ask questions. To give
you a licence to go on here for ever. (*He stops and stares at her*) The work
is so pure—it is invisible! (*He moves round the equipment*) There is
nothing here! That is the truth. Absolutely *nothing*.
Elinor (*calmly, defiantly*) If you say so, that must be right. That must be
correct.
Al (*loudly, powerfully*) And it hurts, doesn't it, when this blundering hack,
somebody who you taught—actually comes along with a fucking good
idea. Out of nowhere, without years of work! This complete mediocrity.
That hurts like hell, doesn't it?

Pause. Elinor puts a nicotine gum in her mouth

What's more, the little bastard can organize things too, can't he! Which
none of you can do. Because you *despise* all that.

Silence

Elinor (*calmly, nicotine gum in her mouth*) For some reason I've always
thought one day you'd probably hurt me. (*She looks across at him*) That
I'd suffer physical harm from you.
Al (*contemptuously*) Don't be ridiculous, that's really ridiculous, Elinor,
isn't it? (*Enraged*) That's truly pathetic.
Elinor Come on, why don't you do what you've come for anyway?
Al Do what?
Elinor Oh, Albie, don't play dumb with me now. You've come to tell me,
that because of the conclusions of the committee that you were a member
of—you are recommending that this department should be closed down,

and the research facilities with it. (*She pauses*) You're not going to hesitate now, are you?

Silence. Al has recovered his calm, watches her for a second

Al I had an idea a few days ago, for a science fiction story, about a nightmare place, a kingdom, where everybody had to sack one person who had been their lover, or best friend. (*He looks at her*) Or someone who they'd hero-worshipped.

Elinor snorts at this

Elinor I should make a note of that if I were you—could be the beginning of your career in fiction. (*She pauses*) So?
Al I will write you a letter.
Elinor A letter? Really? What will it say?

Music

Al (*quietly, carefully*) It will say in view of the present financial realities—this particular university will concentrate on its strengths. And therefore it will no longer possess a chemistry department, no new students will be admitted, and the research facilities will close at the end of September.

Pause

Elinor (*shocked by the date*) September? I need another year, that's too soon.
Al I will send you the letter.
Elinor I need another year, Albie.
Al That is not going to be possible. This is nothing personal, it is happening in many areas.
Elinor (*moving*) I *must* have another year. (*She paces*) If you need evidence … maybe I can let you see something. It's difficult because I'm not ready. I'll have to think about it… I don't know if I can. (*She paces*) It *might* be possible in a few weeks.
Al Elinor, please, it's gone too far.
Elinor Do you want me to apologise?
Al No. *No.*
Elinor I haven't been as well as I usually am—had a little trouble with my health … apologising is something I do very badly. This is about as well as I do it. Maybe I was a little too severe.
Al This is not necessary, please.
Elinor (*suddenly looking straight at him*) You want me to ask in a suitably

humble fashion, do you? Is that what you're after? I will. What do you want
me to do? Tell me.

Al Elinor...

Elinor You're a very pragmatic person, Albie, tell me what I have to do, to
get the closure postponed? (*She pauses and smiles*) Shall I really shock you
and plead...? I will.

Al, clearly embarrassed, turns away

 (*Louder*) Show me what I need to do? (*She watches him*) Show me, Albie.

Ghislane enters

Ghislane Hallo, I just came back to... (*To Elinor, sensing the mood*) I
thought we hadn't had a proper moment to say hallo.

Elinor (*quietly*) No, no, we haven't.

Ghislane Is everything all right?

Elinor Yes—except I'm drinking too much.

Al (*quieter, now they are in public*) I will send you the letter.

Elinor I'm sure you will.

Al (*finding it very awkward, now Ghislane is there*) I know you'll find
alternative funding, I mean with your reputation, there will be no problem.

Elinor And of course at my age, it will be even easier.

Al (*moving very close to her, quietly*) I could make some calls, some
suggestions ... if you want me to.

Elinor No. I do not. You're right, you send me the letter, Albie. I think that's
how it should be. And then you will get my response. (*She moves*) I'm
fairly certain I have never received a letter like that before.

Al (*making to exit*) I will see you before I leave.

Al exits

Pause. The party music playing

Elinor Oh, Jesus! (*She is with her back to Ghislane, shaking, really shaking,
clenched*)

Ghislane Elinor... (*She moves up to her*) I just came, I knew what he was
going to say to you... I wanted to see if you were all right.

Elinor (*loudly, pulling away from her*) Yes. Of course I'm all right. I told you
that. What do you expect me to do—curl up in a heap? (*She pauses*) I didn't
mean to shout, I'm sorry. (*She moves*) I'm not all right, of course, but I will
see to it that I am. (*She stops moving, and her composure begins to return*)
I still have a great desire to finish the work—and that is what is going to
happen. (*Sharply*) Without a doubt—there's plenty of ammunition left...

Ghislane I can't believe we've let him do this to us, Elinor.

Elinor I was not aware I'd *let* him do anything… I even pleaded with him… (*She laughs*) Just now—in my own laboratory—to Albie … to little Albert. (*She moves, with a self-mocking smile*) What's more, I tried—and this is funny—I even tried to demonstrate my "passionate" side to him. (*She laughs*) Oh, yes! To show him I wasn't just a woman of uncertain age, all alone in a prehistoric lab, that there was more to me than tins of barley sugars. (*She mimics herself*) And "supers"… (*She stops moving*) Everything I've done in my life—whatever my achievements are, my reputation, years of work—and it comes down to me pleading with an administrator. To be allowed to exist!

Ghislane Yes. (*She pauses slightly*) And you know Christopher doesn't even hate him.

Elinor Well, at least *he's* been free of Albie's control—since the Occurrence.

Ghislane Well, *I* hate Al. I can't help it. But Christopher glides above it all, refusing to acknowledge anything.

Elinor (*quietly*) He shouldn't be like that. He ought to admit to what's happened. The more he denies it, the more it diminishes him. He must face it, or he'll never be able to restart.

Ghislane I know, I have to make him! I will! (*She moves*) And all the time Al gets more famous. It's extraordinary, his rise, his success. I lie awake at night planning revenge, Elinor, all sorts of scenarios.

Elinor Revenge… (*Lightly*) Certainly, that would be good. But in fact there is no need to worry about that.

Ghislane What do you mean?

Elinor It's already started. A form of revenge. Because Albie has had an original idea.

Ghislane (*with a startled laugh*) I heard that—garbage! That's *revenge*?

Elinor Oh, yes. It's the first fresh idea he's ever had. And now he's thought of it—it almost certainly won't go away. And that will be very unsettling for Albie.

Ghislane I don't see.

Elinor You will. It's simple. (*She looks across at her*) He can't finish it on his own.

Black-out

SCENE 4

Al is alone on stage with a large plastic box at his feet

Behind him is the sound of a Concorde taking off: for a second distant, then passing across the auditorium

Al The bags get bigger, the mementoes smaller. (*He opens a bag and takes out an exhibit*) And in here—what do we have? A sachet of garlic mayonnaise as served on Concorde with king prawns! I'm in Concorde a lot. American freebies.

The plane goes overhead, he blocks his ears

I have had two more pop-science best sellers, the latest called *The End of Hype*—with a big question mark. It has a rather autobiographical thesis— that on one level Science and the Arts, the old Two Cultures argument, have never been further apart, with even the machinery in our homes becoming really difficult to understand. *But* on a deeper level showbiz and science are getting ever closer and closer. (*Beat*) An idea borrowed from Elinor. (*He smiles*) But naturally developed further. (*He moves*) There's a certain fun to be had from hyping a book with a title like that.

The sound changes

And now we're in a helicopter flying across the roof-tops of New York. We're aiming straight towards those great glass buildings like Elinor's Virtual Reality journey, that night. Heading for a reception in an entirely new building, for the launch of a much publicised new book. Not one of mine for once! (*He pauses*) It is the darkest moment of my life so far.

He is handed a plate groaning with food

But the food is great.

Joanna enters

There is the sound of chatter off, as from a cocktail party. A transatlantic twang in Joanna's voice. A pile of shiny books on the floor

Joanna There you are! All alone?
Al That's correct.
Joanna (*laughing at the large plate of food*) But not without ample provisions.
Al Naturally. As always.
Joanna So why did you wander off?
Al I needed to.
Joanna What's wrong? You're normally so gregarious.
Al Because after eight minutes—I'd done that party.
Joanna (*laughing*) Eight minutes! It took as long as that!

Al (*eating*) Only minor celebrities in there.

Joanna You've moved up a league now, have you? Perhaps you have—they have all heard of *you*.

Al (*indicating the shiny pile of books*) And what's more, the book is shit.

Pause. Sound of the cocktail party

Joanna The book is not shit. (*She smiles*) It's fucking fantastic. It's a controversial look at the way we live now, the definitive comment on success, to quote the blurb which I wrote.

Al Oh, come on! We're standing seventy-seven storeys up, celebrating a book about a twelve-year-old boy—who also just happens to be a serial killer. The first child serial killer novel, there had to be one, of course! A perfect book for the dregs of the century.

Joanna You know everything, Al, of course. And the rest of us are just plain dim.

Al I didn't say that. But I can tell you how liquid crystal works, and also read all nine hundred and forty-three pages of this book, and see right through it.

Sounds from the cocktail party. He moves across the stage, tapping sections of the floor

Let me demonstrate something.

Joanna (*nervously*) Demonstrate what?

Al Just have to find the right place. (*He pushes the strip of maroon carpet away*)

Joanna What on earth are you doing?

Al There… (*He lifts up a small piece of the floor*)

Joanna Oh, no, Al, you're not going to start pulling the floor up again. (*She laughs*) You know I still dream about some of the object you conjured up last time you did this.

Al We are in a new building, and what do we find, as in all new buildings? (*He pulls up dark cables from underneath the floor*)

Joanna (*nervously*) What?

Al The whole forest of cables, from the computers, waiting to be connected. (*He pulls up another cable from a second outlet in the floor, and then another, making them stand up so they dot the stage, standing up firmly, like some strange plants*) Look what's underneath your feet, Joanna…!

Joanna Why are they standing up like that?

Al Because I'm making them.

Joanna Snake-charming cables now. They're eerie, Al.

They stare at them

Al And in less than a year you'll see them change shape.

Voices from the party

And those people have no idea what's here, what's in the skirting—do they? In their own offices. (*He moves among the cables*)

Joanna You do at least have one real talent, Al—for producing surprises out of the floor.

Al (*with a lighter tone*) Yes—as *my* blurb says, on *my* dust-jacket, "I have become a detective patrolling the Zeitgeist". (*He is standing still among the cables, his mood darkening*) Idea for a science fiction story—the computer cables in a new office building rustle under the carpets, then they grow, and they rise up, and they strangle the occupants, one by one. What do you think? (*He indicates the books*) It's better already than this shit.

Joanna (*watching him closely*) And this omniscience—does it apply to people too?

Al pushes one of the cables slowly back into its hole

Al People?

Joanna Remember them? You see right through people on first acquaintance? Get accurate printout just by glancing at them?

Al Sometimes, yes.

Joanna And old friends? You know everything there is to know about them too?

Both are moving among the cables, either side of the stage

Al Yes.

Joanna (*touching a cable*) Like Christopher?

Al He lied—wanted to be famous quick.

Joanna That's it? Just that?

Al Yes. The golden boy had a thirst for money and fame, nothing else.

Joanna (*moving to another cable*) And Elinor?

Al Somebody who no longer could compete. A proud lady who couldn't cope with the modern world.

Joanna That's her, is it, too? As simple as that?

Al Yes. Every organization has at least one, a distinguished employee who becomes outmoded.

Joanna She will surprise you yet. And me?

Al You? (*He stares across at her*) I don't think so. (*He turns*)

Joanna Go on. (*She stares at him*) And me?

Slight pause

Al (*calmly*) A funny original woman—who in the end settled for being just another PR nonentity.

Pause

Joanna Fuck you, Al. (*She moves*) Don't you dare tell me I could have done more. I have a career, I have control over my life. I will *not* be judged by you.

Al (*very quietly*) You don't have to believe me.

Joanna You are a complacent little shit, aren't you?

Al (*quietly, darkly*) That's right. Elinor always did say I'd grow up eventually.

Joanna It's rather frightening, the contempt you have.

Al We're all hacks now, Joanna! (*He moves among the cables*) My great mistake was to think I was in a minority. But now we're all the same. (*He glances up at Joanna*) That's why you and I fit the times so perfectly.

Joanna (*fiercely*) It must be marvellous to feel like that, to know you understand absolutely everything.

Al No.

Joanna (*with mock astonishment*) It's not?

Silence. Al is not looking at her

Al You remember I had an idea, Joanna—a great idea.

Joanna Oh, yes, something to do with garbage—how appropriate.

Al Of course, yes. A workable fuel out of refuse, a potentially unlimited supply of energy.

Joanna Sun Garbage in fact!

Al Yes. And I'm sixty per cent of the way there—but I can't make it come out. *Nearly, but I can't.* (*He stares at the cables*) I shut down a department, a department with a great history, but I could go anywhere in the world with it! Find the commitment, build a team. (*He moves*) I wanted to involve Elinor.

Joanna But you didn't have the nerve to ask.

Al I found it impossible to suggest it to her. (*He moves*) I am *tormented* by a good idea, Joanna, that I wish I'd never had! I am in a kind of hell, of planes, parties, bouncing around the world with this in my head. It will not go away!

Joanna So there is some justice then. Driven crazy by your one good idea, not able to finish it—and hopefully it'll never let go of you.

Al Oh, no. (*Very forcefully*) If one thing is certain—there will be a solution.

Joanna (*moving towards the party*) I'm going back in there. I didn't think you could hurt me after all this time, Al, but you have. (*She indicates the* *cables*) I'll leave you with these—with any luck they *will* rise up and start strangling people.

Joanna exits

Al is alone with the cables

In the scene change, the cables slide back into their holes as he watches. The bells ringing loudly in the scene change, celebratory bells

Al exits

SCENE 5

Very strong, bright sunlight

Elinor is sitting c in full red academic robes, smoking

The old Professor is also in academic robes

Barbara is standing US, near the vending machine. She is very tanned, expensively dressed

As the bells stop, we can hear the sound of builders working, sporadic drilling and hammering

Professor That noise! It should not be happening now.

Barbara (*moving round, touching the wall*) Everything seems much smaller than I remember. (*She touches the wall by the old drinks machine*) It all seems to have shrunk.

Professor The builders were meant to stop when the bells started … somebody must see to it before the ceremony.

Barbara (*by the wall*) Was it always this colour? Everything seems more muted—after the West Coast light. (*To Elinor, bending down, raising her voice*) Are you feeling OK? For your big day?

Elinor I'm fine. Feeling tiptop.

Barbara (*bending close*) That's great. And you certainly look it too!

Elinor (*lightly*) Please… Just because I'm getting this honour doesn't mean I've gone deaf suddenly.

Professor It is so *good* this is happening. (*To Barbara*) The Talbot James Award… I think there've only been six other recipients in the whole history of the university—and some of those were undeserved. (*He moves*

to Elinor) You're coming out of the shadow of what Barker-Wyatt did, or
should I say took credit for. At last! No longer in parenthesis, thank God.
Elinor *(with a warm laugh)* Oh, is that where I was all this time? In
parenthesis! I never knew ... that must explain everything.
Professor *(kindly)* What I mean is your wonderful contribution is being
officially acknowledged, long overdue.
Elinor *(lightly, smoking)* Well, we both agree about that. *(She looks at the
Professor)* I don't know how you manage it, Bill, but you look younger all
the time. *(Lightly)* It's infuriating.
Professor It's keeping busy and free of worry. I don't have a single
responsibility any more! *(He moves to Elinor, and taps her on the
shoulder)* We did the hard work, didn't we... *(He indicates Barbara)* All
they have to do is follow the path we mapped out. *(He smiles at Barbara)*
You know Elinor was always startlingly determined, right from the start.
Barbara I bet she was.
Professor We knew we had to be on top form when she was around, or she'd
put us all to shame. We used to call her—I forget why now—we always
used to call her *(he taps Elinor on the shoulder)* the snow tigress.
Elinor Really! *(Very surprised)* I didn't know that...! I quite like it.
Professor Oh, yes. And now this is a very appropriate way for it to end.
Elinor *(turning sharply)* End? Really? Some of us still have work to do.

Professor and Barbara glance at each other. Slight pause

Professor Of course you do, Elinor. I meant the Department ending...
Barbara *(loudly)* Yes. We didn't mean to imply you'd stopped. When do
you think you'll publish?
Elinor Very soon, I hope.
Barbara Good, that's very good. And you've arranged where you're going
next?

A slight awkward pause

You know I've so much room ... several spare rooms, you must come and
visit me in San Diego one day.
Elinor Really? That's very kind. I'd like that very much.
Barbara You would?
Elinor Yes, when can I come? *(She smiles)* I'm free in the autumn.
Barbara *(very taken aback)* So you travel now! You've started flying again?
That's good. That's excellent, well done. We must work something out,
mustn't we?

*Christopher enters with Ghislane. He looks drawn, pale. Ghislane looks
older*

Christopher No need to shout, for God's sake, why are you shouting at her? She's not deaf.

Barbara Was I shouting? I'm sorry. (*With a nervous smile*) Must be the excitement.

Elinor (*to Christopher*) Thank you, much appreciated.

Ghislane (*to Elinor*) Hallo, you look splendid.

Christopher (*smiling fondly*) Of course, she always does. (*He completely ignores Barbara, and moves up to the Professor*) The speeches are usually very embarrassing on these occasions, aren't they? I hope yours will be different.

Professor (*not taking offence*) Well, it will be no more embarrassing than usual. Nor will Albert's. (*He lowers his voice. To Christopher*) I'm anxious we get as good a turn-out as we did for Greenslade. They can vary, you know.

Elinor (*overhearing*) Oh, it's a competition now—who gets the biggest audience for their ceremony! (*She laughs*) Any empty seats will count against me. I'm not really bothered how many people are there, I promise you.

Professor It will be full, I'm sure. It's going to be a fantastic day. Albert has arranged everything so it should go like clockwork.

Ghislane Al can arrange anything, after all!

Ghislane, like Barbara, is nervous, speedy

Christopher I saw Warhurst and Beattie, they looked so much older, I hardly recognized them.

Barbara It's always a bit of an ordeal coming back to a place, after a long gap, isn't it?

Christopher An ordeal, is it? *I'm* not finding it so. I feel no worries at all about facing everybody.

Ghislane Nobody will be thinking about what happened, it's not in anybody's mind.

Christopher Oh, no, on the contrary. I know everybody present will be craning their necks to catch a glimpse—is that really him? How does he look? I don't mind, but it's why a lot of them have come.

Elinor (*amused, smoking*) And here was I thinking today was about me.

Christopher Of course! But some of them *will* arrange to bump into me afterwards. (*He mimics surprise*) "Oh, there you are, Christopher"— hoping for some dramatic confession. (*His eyes meet Ghislane's for a moment*) Which they are never going to get.

Barbara And are you still working?

Christopher (*very sharply*) Of course I'm still working. What do you think I'm doing?

Barbara (*nervously*) No, no, I didn't mean that... I, I, I meant still on the Sun Battery.
Christopher (*with a dismissive wave of the hand*) No, no, you are completely out of date. I've moved on, of course.
Barbara Oh, I see. (*She tries to be friendly*) I knew you would. (*She moves*) Remember the day we had the picnic? I often think about it. I remember it really clearly, there was so much food! We were drowning in it, lots of good cheeses, and the weather was really cold, all the autumn leaves everywhere, getting into everything.
Christopher (*suddenly erupting*) Jesus, you can't even remember that night. Not even that! This is shocking. It was a *summer's day*. A humid day. As if anybody could forget that. You have no memory at all, obviously.

Barbara is totally shocked at this outburst. Silence

Barbara I, I, could have sworn it was a late autumn day. Surely? We were all huddled up in big coats——
Christopher *No*. And you were the one taking the photos! (*Contemptuously*) This is amazing! Or have you forgotten that completely as well?
Professor (*hastily*) Well, there will at least be a good record of today, a video Albert has arranged, at least three cameras I think.
Elinor My Talbot James video! (*She laughs*) Maybe I should collect mementoes like Albie does, something from each of you. (*She looks across at them*) What would you give me?

Al enters, smartly dressed, holding a walkie-talkie

Al It looks like it's going to be a very good turnout!

Elinor laughs

(*Surprised by the reaction*) What's the matter? It's going to be a near record attendance.
Professor Near record? Excellent!
Al (*bringing the cards out*) I have little seating plans for each of you, with your number, showing you where you all need to go.
Christopher You've arranged the entire operation, have you?
Al (*smiling*) Nearly! That building noise shouldn't be going on. (*He speaks into the walkie-talkie*)
Ghislane You can see to that too?
Al (*grinning*) I hope so! I have stewards outside the hall, if they haven't wandered off. (*Into the walkie-talkie*) John, come in ... can you see those builders? They're working on the roof of this building, keep them quiet till the end of the ceremony. Use money, lots if necessary.

Professor Looking after all aspects, splendid!

Al suddenly turns

Al I want you all to go and check your places, now. Just to make sure where they are. (*He looks at Elinor*)
Barbara Already? Why?
Al Then you can come back. Please! *Now!*
Christopher (*calmly*) Of course, Al, whatever you want. (*He begins to move*) The hypocrisy of these occasions—nobody ever says what they're really thinking, do they? All these fulsome addresses, we're *about* to hear, nobody tells the truth.
Professor Thank God. Where would we all be if that happened?
Christopher But wouldn't it be interesting if they really did. Just for once. (*He turns*) If you did, Elinor... *Today!*
Professor Have you all got your seating plans? (*He tries to sound jocular*) Let's follow the instructions then, see how near the front we are!
Al I just have to stay and make sure Elinor is ready.
Elinor (*with a sharp smile*) Oh, is that what has to happen?
Barbara (*as she is moved on*) I really think it's unnecessary for us to do this now. I mean, we're not children! (*She stops by Elinor*) If I don't see you before, good luck.
Elinor Thank you, my dear. (*She looks at Barbara for a second*) You must try and grow a memory, mustn't you?

Barbara exits

Christopher Come on, Ghislane—we will do Albie's check, without complaint. (*Very sharply*) But *I* will be the one who escorts her in. Is that *absolutely* clear? (*To Elinor*) Don't forget what I said, Elinor. (*Softly*) Make it happen.

Christopher exits

Ghislane (*with a nervous laugh*) We're all so dependent now on Al, we even need him to tell us where to sit!

Ghislane exits

The building noise stops

Al There, it's stopped. The noise.
Professor Excellent. (*He moves*) I probably won't recognize this building

next time I come here. *Our* department. It'll have a whole new interior. It
has seen much fine work. All our endeavours, Elinor! But progress has to
have its way. This place's moment has passed. It's unavoidable. It's out of
date. Used up.

Elinor (*lightly*) Are you talking about me, by any chance?

Professor About all of us veterans, my dear. We old contemplators are not
required any more. I include myself. Oh, yes!

Professor exits

Elinor (*pulling on her cigarette*) Like hell he does. (*With a sharp laugh*) And
what's more, he is nearly twenty years older than me! (*She looks across at
Al*)

There's a moment's pause between them

I can't find my hat, Albie. You know, the stupid one with the tassels I like
to wear. And since you're getting me ready…

Al I'll find it. Don't worry—I'll definitely find it. (*He starts searching*)

Elinor (*watching him*) I'm glad it's you in charge of the arrangements today.
First you're being at your most charming—and second it means everything
will work.

Al I hope so. I want it to be a stunning occasion, beautiful. (*Quietly*) One of
the best days of our lives.

Elinor (*after a slight pause*) Of course. (*She takes a drag and blows smoke*)
But Christopher is right.

Al (*surprised*) Christopher's right? About what?

Elinor That nobody tells the truth on these occasions.

Al But surely it'd be awful if they did.

Elinor It's like obituaries—they never tell the truth either. (*With a calm
smile*) Have you written my obituary yet?

Al (*startled*) Elinor, what a question! Don't be stupid…

Elinor No, come on now, tell me. I'm sure you've done one for a "serious"
newspaper. After all… (*She laughs*) They always do them early for people
who smoke a lot. And since I'm on eighty a day now, I'm sure to have one!
(*Softly*) What's it like, Albie?

Al (*with a nervous laugh*) We can't have this conversation!

Elinor Oh, yes, we can.

Slight pause

Al It's good. You'd like it, I think.

Elinor (*with a slow smile*) So you *have* written one?

Al Yes.

Elinor (*laughing*) I can guess what you've said—keep looking for the hat please.

Al Yes. (*As he looks*) I have said this was—is—the life of an important and tremendously gifted scientist, of course! A truly pure practitioner.

Elinor I don't want to hear the *mush*, I can imagine that, very easily. But what should you have said? That's much more interesting. (*She looks straight at him*) And what should you jolly well have the guts to say today—instead of all the deadly politeness I'm going to get.

Al I should say... (*After a slight pause he looks up*) My teacher, my idol, had one great lapse when she tried to gloss over an incident of serious scientific misconduct—and things were never the same again.

Elinor You definitely should say it, during the ceremony. I dare you, Albert.

Al Many, many time I've wondered... (*Suddenly urgent*) Why did you do that?

Elinor (*calmly smoking*) That's not difficult—because I was frightened of you.

Al Oh, come on! That's not true!

Elinor Oh, yes... (*She smiles*) Keep looking for the hat—the idea of having to justify my performance, that was alarming. (*She moves*) I knew Christopher would be able to save me from all that, *once* he'd achieved his work.

Al I don't believe you! I can't believe you were frightened! (*Suddenly, on an impulse, he moves over to the lockers*) This is *not* a serious idea, OK! But maybe we can see something. *Don't laugh*—you promise.

Elinor I don't promise anything.

Al (*by the lockers*) There was a moment recently, when I saw things very clearly. But now... (*He is opening the lockers, bulging with transparent bags*)

Elinor laughs at the sight of them

Elinor Oh, no, not those wretched bags again, Albie, please!

Al Oh, yes! Eventually I took over all these lockers, as they became vacant. (*He begins to pull the bags out and they stream out*) They're spooky, I know, eccentric, yes, a schoolboy habit retained.

The bags are in long glistening lines, tied together, stretching out across the stage

But here they are. (*He grins*) And if we're not going to be *polite*—then we can use them.

Elinor God, how many did you keep!

Al It's all here. I colour-coded them recently... (*He smiles*) My passion for order. There's blue for when I was very young and——

Elinor And I started teaching you.

Al Yes, and over there, gold for when Christopher made his "great" discovery.

Elinor And then *red* for everything that followed.

Al Yes! (*He moves to the glistening lines, beginning to move them to form a pattern*) So look, Elinor—look! They form a crude diagram, you see, an instant pattern of the past.

Elinor They won't help. They can't show us anything.

Al They will, they can! We can form any configuration with them—*show why what happened, did. Cause* and *effect*.

Elinor (*staring at the lines of bags, with a sharp laugh*) People will come in from the Assembly Hall and find us playing with plastic bags!

Al holds up a bag

Al Look, Elinor—look at this one—it's the day I became a professor, it's caught in here, takes you right back to that moment, instantaneously! Do you remember that afternoon?

Elinor Yes, of course. Your nosebleed and your new shoes.

Al (*holding up a bag*) There is the blood-stained handkerchief right there.

Elinor (*staring fascinated for a moment*) So it is. And I never saw you have another nosebleed, after that day.

Al I know, remarkable what a little confidence will do. (*He moves along the lines, changing the pattern, moving the blue and the black together*) So is the key to everything—*watch*—what happened on that sleepy day? Did I actually *scheme* to stop you becoming Head of the Department, you and Christopher?

Elinor Yes and no. Nothing is that simple.

Music from the hall begins, slow, ceremonial

Al I didn't! I really don't believe I did. I was only trying to survive that interview, to give the old bastard the answers he wanted.

Elinor (*softly*) And you did that brilliantly, Albie, as always. Forever adaptable. (*She flinches at the sound of the music*) Listen to that pompous music—they only give you these lifetime achievement awards when they think you're no longer a threat... (*With a sharp laugh*) When they believe you're already half-dead.

Al moves the shape of the diagram

What are you doing? Try as hard as you can, you cannot reduce what happened to one neat pattern.

Al Oh, yes. *Everything is reducible in the end*, if you find the key, and I can.

(*He moves along the line*) We can follow the trail ... watch ... through this first day when there were stirrings of resentment and jealousy, because it was the hack that got the job.

Elinor No, that's wrong. Too crude. Because you're not just a hack, Albert. That has never been the case.

Al looks up very startled. Pause

Al I don't think you've ever said that to me before.

Elinor Haven't I? I'm sure I must have ... in different words.

Al No. Not ever.

Elinor You were one of the brighter people that I taught. You stood out, one of the quickest minds of all. (*She moves*) What does it matter now? (*With a slight laugh*) Not much can change, can it—now, unless I can get out of today, somehow.

Al So here is the vital one—the gold—the great day of Christopher's announcement. (*Suddenly urgent*) And I know why he *did it*, now. It wasn't just fame, was it? The primary cause. It wasn't money...

Elinor (*amused*) Probably not the primary cause, Albie, no.

Al Elinor, please don't mock. I know, because I've been there as well.

Elinor Where, Albie?

Al The hell of creating something. That is, in the dark tunnel you have to be in. *There is the key!* Christopher couldn't do it because he couldn't be there long enough. He lasted of course much longer than I did. But it snapped. He got so close, upsettingly close, but *something* had eaten away at his stamina. He couldn't bear to be there any more. In that *darkness*. (*He stares across at her*) You don't have that problem, Elinor, do you?

Elinor (*lightly smoking*) This is true—I do not.

Al The long-distance creator, maybe an endangered species...

Pause

Is that even nearly right, do you think?

Elinor I'm sure it's one of the aspects, yes, Albie.

Al (*loudly*) One of the aspects! Don't do that, it's the *truth*. Because I know— I've felt it.

Ghislane enters

Ghislane I forgot our number. Your seating plan. (*She picks her way across the bags, staring at them*) Oh, Al—taking these with you? (*She laughs*) Your unique diary. (*She finds the seating plan*) Here it is. (*She moves, then turns to Elinor*) Elinor, I can't bear the idea of facing them all. I know what they'll be thinking.

Elinor It will be fine, I'm sure. (*Then slightly embarrassed*) Nobody will be thinking about it.

Ghislane It will be fine for *Christopher*, I'm sure. He still refuses to acknowledge anything. But for me? You know the picnic that Barbara mentioned. I still have copies of the pictures she took. And the striking thing is—Christopher looks exactly the same now, as he did on that day. It all shows on me, not just my hair, but everything about me, I can feel it when people meet me, they see it all on me! However much I smile and chirp away, they sense it at once. (*Louder*) And that's never going to change now, is it? (*To both of them*) And you know it's not. (*Intensely*) That's what I've got now. (*She moves and glances at Elinor*) You *do* look wonderful. (*She takes a deep breath*) Here goes.

Ghislane exits

Elinor (*with feeling*) Poor girl.

Al is quiet. Elinor stares across the lines

Where is *that picnic*? The celebratory picnic you didn't attend, Al. That day must be here, scrunched up somewhere.

Al It's just here… (*He gives Elinor the bag*) And it's the other great pointer, isn't it? The day when we argued, when you told me to do nothing, which led *directly* to the most stupid decision of my life. (*He moves the red line across*) Which I wish I could redraw. *Closing you down.*

Elinor Yes. (*She surveys the lines*) It's a haunting shape, Albie.

Al And it's right.

Elinor There is one problem. (*She smiles*) If we're going to use these comic things. (*She moves them with her foot*)

Al Yes, you use them. (*He grins*) We're working together, for really the first time!

Elinor Don't you see, Albie, none of this is the real pattern of what happened. The *only* shape we can be definite about is… (*She picks a bag at random*) Or indeed this… (*She chucks it away and picks up another*)

Al What is it? I don't understand.

Elinor They're all *you*, Albie. The only thing we know for certain is… (*She pushes the solitary bag along the stage with her foot*) You were always, *always* going to close me down. Whatever happened.

Al (*immediately*) No! That is not right.

Elinor Oh, yes! Without Christopher's aberration, and the way I "shocked" you, without any of that taking place—you would still undoubtedly have done it.

Al You're absolutely wrong.

Elinor (*straight at him*) And of course you would do it *again*. Tomorrow if necessary, with no compunction at all. (*She stares at him*) Maybe even quicker.

Al No, for Chrissake, Elinor! Are you saying I've learnt nothing. Because that's not true.

Elinor You would do it again for a simple reason—you don't know what I'm doing. And mystery is expensive, infuriating, and uneconomic...

Al Oh, come on, Elinor!

Elinor I will not compromise, even now. And you hate me for that.

Al (*shocked*) Elinor.

Elinor Oh, yes.

Al I have never hated you. This is rubbish. I admire you more than anybody, passionately, with something akin to love. Of course you must know that.

Elinor You'd still shut me down, Albie. No problem, as the kids say. Wouldn't you?

Pause. She looks across at him

You see.

Silence. She smiles

And what you don't know—and now I'm going to be outrageous, even more arrogant than usual, what you have no idea about... Was I—am I—the future?

Al is quiet, shaken, watching her

(*Turning towards the music, shivering slightly*) I wish they'd stop playing that horrible music, though. (*She smokes*) Termination music...

Al (*quietly, slowly*) Elinor, you know the idea, my garbage proposal. (*He smiles*) The Sun Garbage, do you remember?

Elinor Yes, it was a super idea.

Al I cannot make it come out. And I cannot create the circumstances where I feel I'm going to get there. I have abandoned it. (*He looks at her*) We should have worked together. Imagine what we could have done! With my admin and your genius. (*Louder*) Why did we never work together?

Elinor Because this was not the time.

Al What do you mean by that? If I'd asked you that day, when I had the chance, to form the unit with me, I *ought* to have asked you!

Elinor It would have made no difference. I'm very fond of you, Albie. (*Steely*) But I would have never wanted to work with you, under any circumstances.

Pause

Al Jesus, Elinor… (*He pauses*) Even today … you're so implacable.
Elinor Yes.

Pause. She watches him for a moment

Now find the hat.
Al (*with a nervous laugh*) Of course. (*He moves among the bags*) It's got
more difficult now!
Elinor Maybe this is the way I can avoid the ceremony. (*She mimics*) The
old bastard intoning "it is our great and long overdue pleasure to honour
our colleague" and I'm *not there*! I'll get in my car and sail out of here, why
not? (*She looks at Al*) Perhaps we should, Albie, get in the old Morris and
escape.
Al Great idea.
Elinor Yes, it is. (*Suddenly with feeling*) Oh, God, I wish I could!

Pause, the music changes

That sounds ominous, doesn't it. (*With a nervous laugh she moves along
the bench. Suddenly she's very nervous, now it's so close*) I was sitting
here, on this very bench, on my first day in this building, still a schoolgirl,
waiting for my interview. It'll be full of media students very soon. (*She
laughs*) It's very appropriate, everything I've spent my time filtering out
of my life … coming here in a big hurry.

*Al picks up a bag from the centre of the stage. It contains an empty tin of baked
beans. He rips it open. Elinor is US, smoking*

Al (*very precisely*) Elinor died eighteen months later, in a way she would
have approved of, might even have delighted her. She suddenly keeled
over while shopping one day. She was carrying, tantalisingly, three boxes
of A4 paper, as if she was preparing to set something down. She still
worked on a 1950s Olivetti. But there was nothing typed yet. Without
access to a lab—she hadn't quite finished. (*He smiles*) Her handwritten
notes were infuriatingly indecipherable, naturally. I *tried* but they were
dense, spidery, secret. The builders have finished the renovation. But the
building is standing empty, because of an inter-departmental row about
finance. There is just silence here, of course, and the gradually fading smell
of new paint in the passages.

Christopher enters abruptly

Christopher Come on, it's time. For Chrissake, what have you been doing
in here? It's her entrance *now*. She's going to be late.

Al Shit! Yes! But we haven't been able to find the hat.
Elinor Doesn't matter, Albie. (*She laughs*) My one anarchic gesture—to enter bareheaded!
Christopher Give them a shock, good. I can't believe those faces in there. They're so predictable. They *are* all craning their necks to look at me. What does a disgraced scientist look like? It really *is* an ordeal—even worse than I thought. I'm terrified. After today I'm never coming back. But I had to be here for this, Elinor. (*To Al*) You want to take her in?
Al No, you take Elinor. That's how it should be.
Christopher Or all three of us in a row? (*He smiles*) Make a bigger splash!
Al No. I'm quite happy. I'll be right behind. (*He grins*) But don't say where I belong.
Elinor No. We won't. Not today. (*Quite anxious to know the answer*) Is it as good a turnout as Albie says?
Christopher Better!

Al helps straighten Elinor's robes, as Elinor smiles

Al We can whisper as we go down the aisle, to ease the tension.
Elinor Whisper what?
Al I don't know … about the weather. (*Softly*) Or what your work really is! What a time to tell!
Elinor (*laughing*) That's a good try, Albie, one of your very best.
Al (*suddenly*) Shit! Where are the bells? Come on … come on! They should have started. At least then today will *seem* complete. (*He reaches for the walkie-talkie*) I may have to see to this——

But the bells start, just as he's about to go into action

Ah, we made it!
Elinor Good. I knew you would arrange it well, Albie.

Pause

Christopher Right! Everybody ready? One, two, three…

Christopher exits

Al is about to, he turns. Elinor has not moved

Al (*impatiently*) Elinor? What are you doing? Come on.
Elinor Patience. (*She takes a drag*) I'm coming. (*She looks across at him*)

The Lights fade

FURNITURE AND PROPERTY LIST

Further dressing may be added at the director's discretion

ACT I

SCENE 1

On stage: UNIVERSITY SCIENCE DEPARTMENT:
Crumbling emblem
Bench seats. *On one*: cup of tea and tin of ginger biscuits
Row of full-length old wooden lockers. *In one of them*: transparent
plastic bags, one with faded colour supplement, another with
cinema ticket; jacket
Old-fashioned soft drinks machine
Old tannoy
Phone

Off stage: Mug of tea (**Christopher**)
Large desk with papers leaking out of its drawers (**SM**)

Personal: **Al:** jacket, handkerchief
Elinor: cigarette
Joanna: chocolate

SCENE 2

On stage: UNIVERSITY SCIENCE DEPARTMENT

Set: Chair
Plastic bag containing coloured paper strips
Papers

Off stage: Sneakers, shoulder bag (**Joanna**)
Cardboard charts, another plastic bag containing a glass (**Al**)

Personal: **Al:** jacket

SCENE 3

On stage: Black metal Virtual Reality car with its joystick and VR headset
Shopping-mall chairs
Milkshakes

Personal: **Elinor:** cigarette paper and tobacco

SCENE 4

On stage: UNIVERSITY SCIENCE DEPARTMENT

Set: Plastic bag containing half-empty tin of barley sugars, fragment of
child's picture

Off stage: Simple wooden table with metal stand and clamp holding glass tube
(**Barbara** and **SM**)
Rolled-up picture (**SM**)
Service area of cafeteria, table with upturned chairs (**SM**)

Personal: **Elinor:** tin of barley sugars

SCENE 5

On stage: UNIVERSITY SCIENCE DEPARTMENT

Set: Plastic bag containing Sainsbury's Baking Powder
Recess in floor containing strangely-shaped fragments of broken
scientific equipment, old jars of chemicals, tin of baking powder,
bleach
Panel in side of stage containing spooky old canisters, large metal
fragments, piles of yellowing papers

SCENE 6

On stage: UNIVERSITY SCIENCE DEPARTMENT

Set: Plastic bag containing ear plugs

Off stage: Baskets of food (**Barbara**)
Baskets groaning with food including bag of grapes (**Christopher**
and **Ghislane**)
Bag containing notebook (**Joanna**)

Personal: **Elinor:** cigarette paper and tobacco

ACT II

SCENE 1

On stage: UNIVERSITY SCIENCE DEPARTMENT

Set: Larger plastic container with audio tapes, press cuttings, fork
               Deep armchairs

SCENE 2

On stage: UNIVERSITY SCIENCE DEPARTMENT

Set: New vending machine
               Cafeteria tables. *On one of them*: upturned chairs
               Service area
               Pudding bowl containing custard
               Bigger bowl of custard
               Formica table
               Ladle
               Baked beans
               Mushy peas
               Very overcooked burgers
               Sweetcorn
               Chips
               Cloth

Off stage: Large black rubbish bag stuffed with papers (**Al**)

SCENE 3

On stage: UNIVERSITY SCIENCE DEPARTMENT

Set: Portion of **Elinor**'s scientific apparatus
               Bottle of whisky
               China cups
               Practical lamps

Off stage: Tape recorder (**Ghislane**)
               Battered old tin (**Elinor**)

Personal: **Elinor:** nicotine gum

Scene 4

On stage: Plastic box
Bag containing airline food
Pile of shiny books
Maroon carpet
Dark cables

Off stage: Plate groaning with food (**SM**)

Scene 5

On stage: University Science Department

Set: Vending machine
Lockers bulging with transparent bags
Bag containing tin of baked beans

Off stage: Walkie-talkie (**Al**)
Seating cards (**Al**)

Personal: **Elinor:** cigarette

LIGHTING PLOT

Practical fittings required: lamps
Various interior and exterior settings

ACT I, Scene 1

To open: Overall general lighting

Cue 1   **Al**: "It's a bloody nightmare."   (Page 9)
             Black-out

ACT I, Scene 2

To open: Overall general lighting

Cue 2   **Elinor** exits   (Page 14)
             Change lights to neon light along back wall

Cue 3   **Al**: "…possibly—begins to form."   (Page 15)
             Black-out

ACT I, Scene 3

To open: Neon light

Cue 4   **Elinor**: "…takes me out for a night on the town!"   (Page 21)
             Black-out

ACT I, Scene 4

To open: Overall general lighting

Cue 5   Muzak starts up   (Page 23)
             Fade lights down

Cue 6   Muzak swells up   (Page 23)
            Bring up beam of light across darkened stage

Cue 7   **Joanna** and **Barbara** exit   (Page 24)
            Bring overall lights back on

Cue 8   **SM** move apparatus off   (Page 26)
            Change lighting to strong sunlight

Cue 9   **Al**: "...more information out of him, somehow."   (Page 31)
            Black-out

ACT I, SCENE 5

To open: Overall general lighting

Cue 10   **Al** pushes debris violently into hole   (Page 37)
            Black-out

ACT I, SCENE 6

To open. Overall general lighting

Cue 11   **Al**: "...to keep mementoes of lack of sleep."   (Page 37)
            Bring up early morning light

Cue 12   **Al**: "Evil old sod!"   (Page 39)
            Make lights brighter

Cue 13   **Al**: "Rumble me!"   (Page 50)
            Fade lights down

ACT II, SCENE 1

To open: Overall general lighting

Cue 14   **Joanna**: "That's a little better."   (Page 55)
            Black-out

ACT II, SCENE 2

To open: Overall lighting; vending machine neon display on

Cue 15   **Al**: "...working in unison for the first time."   (Page 61)
            Black-out

ACT II, SCENE 3

To open: Reddening sun effect, going down during the scene, and various
            lamps switched on

Cue 16   **Elinor**: "He can't finish it on his own."   (Page 74)
            Black-out

ACT II, SCENE 4

To open: Overall general lighting

No cues

ACT II, SCENE 5

To open: Very strong, bright sunlight

Cue 17   **Elinor** looks across at **Al**   (Page 91)
            Fade lights down

EFFECTS PLOT

ACT I

Cue 1   Lights change   (Page 14)
          Shopping-mall muzak in background

Cue 2   To open Scene 3   (Page 15)
          Muzak, continuing, and intermittent sound of sudden,
              heavy, pulsating noise of money pouring out of arcade
              machines

Cue 3   **Elinor** puts headset on stage   (Page 17)
          Sound of money pouring out of arcade machines

Cue 4   **Al**: "…something you'd never normally do."   (Page 17)
          Bring up sound of sirens in distance

Cue 5   **Elinor**: "Reminding me of my age!"   (Page 17)
          Sound of money pouring out of arcade machines

Cue 6   **Al**: "As you talk brilliant science."   (Page 18)
          Bring up clamour of burglar alarms in distance,
              continuing

Cue 7   **All** look at **Al** in surprise   (Page 18)
          Bring up urban night sounds to full

Cue 8   **Joanna**: "Like hell you did!"   (Page 19)
          Sound of amusement arcades

Cue 9   **Joanna**: "I'll remember what I'm wearing!"   (Page 23)
          Muzak

Cue 10 **Barbara** supervises as equipment is brought in   (Page 23)
          Increase muzak to full, coming from elsewhere in the
              building, a radio blaring out light orchestral music

Cue 11	A beam of light stabs across darkened stage *Start bubbling effect in tube*	(Page 23)
Cue 12	**Al** switches tannoy on *Bring up buzz of expectant chattering over tannoy,* *gradually building louder and louder, then*	(Page 26)
Cue 13	**Charlie**: "In every sense." **Christopher**'s *voice over tannoy as script page 26*	(Page 26)
Cue 14	**Al** switches tannoy off *Cut tannoy sounds*	(Page 27)
Cue 15	**Al** switches tannoy on *Voices over tannoy as script page 28*	(Page 28)
Cue 16	**Ghislane** switches tannoy off *Cut tannoy sounds*	(Page 29)
Cue 17	**Ghislane** turns up tannoy *Tannoy sounds of people beginning to move and* **Christopher**'s *voice as script page 30*	(Page 30)
Cue 18	**Al** begins to throw objects out of hole *Bring up some Bach music drifting from somewhere* *deep in building*	(Page 31)
Cue 19	**Al** sits at his large desk *Bring up sound of birdsong, radios in distance,* *continuing*	(Page 39)
Cue 20	**Al**: "Elinor?" *Sound of people playing computer games in nearby* *rooms, continuing*	(Page 44)
Cue 21	**Elinor**: "Albie, calm down … please." *After pause, prolonged burst of computer games sounds*	(Page 45)
Cue 22	**Elinor**: "You still do nothing." *Zigzagging sound of computers, then silence*	(Page 46)
Cue 23	**Elinor** looks at **Al** *Burst of computer games sound outside*	(Page 47)

Cue 24   **Elinor**: "You must not do it."   (Page 48)
          Computer sounds, lazy rhythms, music drifting

ACT II

Cue 25   **Al**: "It could be fantastic."   (Page 59)
          *Bring up **Elinor**'s music in distance*

Cue 26   To open Scene 3   (Page 61)
          Faint sounds of students' parties, from other buildings,
          gentle noise of distant music

Cue 27   **Al**: "This is terrific … Elinor, isn't it?"   (Page 68)
          Slightly increase sound of parties

Cue 28   **Elinor**: "…thing you've come to tell me, Albie."   (Page 70)
          Bring up more new music and party sounds

Cue 29   **Elinor**: "What will it say?"   (Page 72)
          Slightly change party music again

Cue 30   **Al** exits   (Page 73)
          Slightly change party music

Cue 31   To open Scene 4   (Page 74)
          Sound of Concorde taking off in distance, approaching

Cue 32   **Al**: "American freebies."   (Page 75)
          Sound of Concorde passing overhead

Cue 33   **Al**: "…hyping a book with a title like that."   (Page 75)
          Change sound of receding Concorde to helicopter
          sound, then fade

Cue 34   **Joanna** enters   (Page 75)
          Bring up sound of cocktail party chatter, off

Cue 35   **Al**: "And what's more, the book is shit."   (Page 76)
          Slightly change sound of cocktail party

Cue 36   **Al**: "…and see right through it."   (Page 76)
          Slightly change sound of cocktail party

Cue 37   **Al**: "...you'll see them change shape."   (Page 77)
            Voices from party

Cue 38   During scene change to Scene 5   (Page 79)
            *Slide cables back in holes, bring up celebratory bells
              ringing loudly*

Cue 39   To open Scene 5   (Page 79)
            *Cut bells, bringing up sound of builders working,
              sporadic drilling and hammering*

Cue 40   **Ghislane** exits   (Page 83)
            Cut building noises

Cue 41   **Elinor**: "Nothing is that simple."   (Page 86)
            Bring up slow, ceremonial music from hall

Cue 42   **Elinor**: "Oh, God, I wish I could!"   (Page 90)
            Change music

Cue 43   **Al**: "I may have to see to this——"   (Page 91)
            Bring up bells ringing